The Teacher Development Series

The
Language
Teacher's
Voice

HEINEMANN
English Language Teaching

Macmillan Heinemann English Language Teaching
Between Towns Road, Oxford OX4 3PP
A division of Macmillan Publishers Limited
Companies and representatives throughout the
world

ISBN 0 333 91650 6

Designed by eMC Design
Series design by Mike Brain
Illustrated by Patrick Williams
Cover picture: Chladni plate, courtesy of the
University of British Columbia

The author and publishers would like to thank the
following for permission to reproduce copyright
material:
Doroth Aldis © 1967 G.P. Putnam's sons for 'The
Nose', p22; Alan Duff for the poems on pp33/34;
John Masefield for the poem on p36; Hilaire Belloc
for 'Henry King', p42; Ted Hughes for 'King of
Carrion', Faber and Faber Ltd p46;

Roger McGough for '40/Love', p48;
Peter Appleton for 'The Responsibility', p49.

The sources of the poem at the bottom of p35, the
two poems at the top of p36, the poem on p44 and
the play extract on p43 are unknown. It has not
been possible to trace the copyright holders of all
material used, and in such cases the publishers
would welcome information from them.

The author and publishers wish to acknowledge the
following sources for activities in this book:
Michael McCallion/Faber & Faber: *Conducting the
orchestra*, p9; Kristin Linklater/Drama Book
Publishers: *Vacuuming the lungs*, p10; Mario
Rinvolucri: questionnaire, p19; Goodith White/
OUP; *The tell-tale voice*, p20; Dalton and
Seidlhofer/OUP: *How do they sound?*, p21; Tim
Murphey: *Shadowing*, p22; Adrian Underhill: *The
inner workbench*, p23; Bernard Dufeu/OUP: *Guided
relaxation*, p24; Chris Brewer and Don Campbell/
Zephyr Press: *The owl*, p27; Cynthia Beresford:
How to say it, p42; Cicely Berry/Virgin Books:
Stretching the text 1, p44; Patsy Rodenburg/
Methuen: *The Actor Speaks*, p45; Kristen Linklater/
Theatre Communications Group: *Breaking down
and building up*, p46; Jim Kahny: *Star for a day*, p47;
Stephen Cheng/Destiny Books: *Tao exercises*,
pp55–8; Don Campbell/ Theosophical Publishing
House: *Thinking the sound*, p59; Don Campbell/
Theosophical Publishing House, Olivea Dewhurst-
Maddock/Gaia Books, Kay Gardner/Element
Books: *Mantras*, p64

Printed in China

2004 2003 2002 2 01 20 0
10 9 8 7 6 5 4 3 2 1

Contents

About the author

I have been involved in English Language Teaching now for over 35 years, so I have been lucky to live through all the many changes which have taken place during that period. I worked for the British Council until 1988 in a variety of countries, including Yugoslavia, Ghana, Italy, France, China and India. I resigned from the British Council in 1988 to take up the post of Director-General of the Bell Educational Trust in Cambridge, where I stayed until 1993. After that I went to the National University of Singapore for five years as Senior Fellow. Now I divide my time between Assumption University, Bangkok, where I have set up a new MA in ELT, and freelance consultancy and writing. It has been a fascinating life! I have always been interested in the human side of language learning rather than the academic or technical aspects. What makes learners and teachers tick, how teachers create a supportive learning atmosphere, how both learners and teachers draw on their creative capacities – these are the kinds of things I have been most concerned with. Working with teachers' voices is, for me at least, a natural extension of these interests. I am in awe of the beauty and complexity of the human voice, the most subtle of all instruments. So I have been amazed at our failure to give teachers any help with developing and protecting their most valuable asset: their voice. Hence this book.

Alan Maley

…what a strange thing the human voice is, this tiny instrument in the throat, with its hidden universe of notes, its delicate, inscrutable laws.
Amit Chaudhuri

The Teacher Development Series

TEACHER DEVELOPMENT is the process of becoming the best teacher you can be. It means becoming a student of learning, your own as well as that of others. It represents a widening of the focus of teaching to include not only the subject matter and the teaching methods, but also the people who are working with the subject and using the methods. It means taking a step back to see the larger picture of what goes on in learning, and how the relationship between students and teachers influences learning. It also means attending to small details which can in turn change the bigger picture. Teacher development is a continuous process of transforming human potential into human performance, a process that is never finished.

The Teacher Development Series offers perspectives on learning that embrace topic, method and person as parts of one larger interacting whole. We aim to help you, the teacher, trainer or academic manager to stretch your awareness not only of what you do and how you do it, but also of how you affect your learners and colleagues. This will enable you to extract more from your own experience, both as it happens and in retrospect, and to become more actively involved in your own continuous learning. The books themselves will focus on new treatments of familiar subjects as well as areas that are just emerging as subjects of the future.

The series represents work that is in progress rather than finished or closed. The authors are themselves exploring, and invite you to bring your own experience to the study of these books while at the same time learning from the experiences of others. We encourage you to observe, value and understand your own experience, and to evaluate and integrate relevant external practice and knowledge into your own internal evolving model of effective teaching and learning.

Adrian Underhill

Other titles in the Teacher Development Series

Children Learning English	Jayne Moon
Inside Teaching	Tim Bowen Jonathan Marks
Learning Teaching	Jim Scrivener
Readings in Teacher Development	Katie Head Pauline Taylor
Sound Foundations	Adrian Underhill
The ELT Manager's Handbook	Graham Impey Nic Underhill

Introduction to *The Language Teacher's Voice*

Nothing remains but the human voice, this tiny instrument inside the throat endeavouring to carry a world inside it.
Amit Chaudhuri

Why a book on voice?

- Because, quite simply, we are our voices. Our individual voiceprints are every bit as distinctive as, and a great deal more public than, our fingerprints. (See the second activity on p viii.) Others judge us by them. It is through our voices that we tell others who – and how – we are. It is surely in our own interests to become aware of how we sound, and to change it if we wish to do so.
- Because, by developing a confident, natural speaking voice, which can sustain prolonged use, we have the capacity to change our relationships with our students. A tired voice conveys a lack of enthusiasm which students pick up on immediately. A richly textured voice, resonant with confidence and vitality, raises the energy levels of those who come into contact with it.
- Because, through better understanding and control of our own voices, we can share the benefits of voicework with our students. This has the double benefit of making them both more confident and more motivated to learn.

You might well object that we already know how to use our voices. After all, we have been doing so since childhood. So what is the problem? Yet like so much else in our lives, we tend to take our voices for granted. And what we take for granted, we neglect. In the case of teachers, we neglect our voices at our peril.

Just consider for a moment how much time you spend each day talking, and the kinds of talking you do. If you are working with a teacher development group, make a list and compare it with others in the group.

As teachers, we rely on our voices to a prodigious degree. For much of the time, we are 'on stage' in a public arena, with all that that entails in terms of stress and expenditure of nervous energy. Yet despite this heavy reliance on our voices, there is virtually no systematic training for teachers in the effective use of the voice.

Actors, who use their voices professionally for a good deal less time than teachers, are given rigorous training in voice use over three years or more, and continue to carry out voicework on a regular basis throughout their careers. Other professional voice users, such as politicians and business executives, regularly seek voice training (and pay a lot of money for it!). But teachers continue to take their most precious asset, their voice, for granted.

One of the effects of this neglect is sustained overuse and misuse of our voices, which impairs our efficiency and may even cause permanent damage. There is now a great deal of evidence to show that teachers suffer more than most professionals from a number of voice-related symptoms. These may range from reduced vocal range or volume to chronic hoarseness or even total voice loss.

It is difficult to think of any other injury that individuals pay as little attention to as voice injury.
Martin and Darnley

Activity: Voice scan

How many of these statements are true for you?

1. My voice gets tired quickly.
2. I sometimes run out of breath when I am speaking.
3. I often get a sore throat after speaking for a long time.
4. I need to clear my throat quite a lot.
5. I don't think my voice sounds as good as it used to.
6. My throat often feels dry after I have been speaking for some time.
7. I sometimes experience a kind of tightness in the throat muscles.
8. My voice often sounds tired and dead, lacking energy.
9. I have difficulty making myself heard when speaking to large groups.
10. I wish I had a more attractive voice.

Even if only a few of these are true for you, you can benefit from using this book!

Although we may not have developed serious voice malfunctions, we may still be operating below our potential best. You can probably recall teachers from your own past who brought life and colour to their classes through the quality of their voices – and others whose voices gave the kiss of death to what they were teaching.

This concern for voice quality should arguably be developed to an even greater degree among teachers of language. The current obsession with fluent communication in foreign language learning is in danger of obscuring the need to develop a feel for the physical substance of the language, its characteristic rhythm, its muscular energy, its visceral undercurrents and its aesthetic appeal. This is something we, as teachers, can convey through our voices.

Activity: Your voice profile

- Think of someone you know well. It may be a public figure, or someone you know personally. Use the list below to characterize their voice. Mark the adjectives with a tick or a cross. If you are not sure, put a question mark. At the end, make a list of all the ticked items; this is the voice profile of your 'subject'. If you are working in a group, discuss your judgements with others.

- Now complete the list for yourself. If you are working with a group, check whether other members agree with your self-perceptions. If you are working on your own, try to find someone who knows you well to check with.

muffled	shrill	breathy	strangled	nasal	bubbly
strained	nervous	booming	squeaky	forced	tired
purring	gravelly	thin	whining	quavery	clear
husky	resonant	velvety	mature	vibrant	lilting
deep	dead	flat	friendly	throaty	slurred

The profile you get from the previous activity is where you are starting from. You may wish to do the activity again after working on your voice for a few months and compare the two profiles.

All of us have the potential to develop powerful, confident and sensitive voices. But this potential will only be realized if we take action to develop it. This book is intended to help you do just that.

> *What we are is to a large extent what we make ourselves.*
> Michael McCallion

Some important issues

1 Everything is habit

Infants do what comes naturally. They have a poise and balance which we lose as we 'mature' and acquire habits which change the natural use of our bodies. The kind of chairs we sit on, the beds we sleep in, the repetitive routines of work, the parental admonitions to 'sit up straight', the adaptations we bring about in our body use in response to stress and injury ... all serve to distort our natural body use into a habitual pattern. Voice is just one of the faculties which suffers as a result.

The problem is that habits, just because they are habitual, feel 'normal'. And what is natural will therefore feel abnormal, at least to begin with:

> *... even when we do try to realign ourselves, the body 'prefers' the old*
> *pattern, in fact it rejects the new posture as wrong because it identifies*
> *and is comfortable with the old habitual position.*
> Martin and Darnley

Therefore, you must not expect work on the voice to be easy. Neither are there any quick fixes. To change habits takes time and regular, sustained hard work. The profit in it is that, if you can re-establish natural use, you will be able to exercise choice in how you use your body (including your voice). Habit leaves you no choice but to continue the habitual pattern.

It is also a fact that, by changing your habitual patterns of use, you yourself will change. In some sense, you will become another person. But be reassured – all those I have worked with have preferred their new self to the habit-shackled self they have left behind.

2 Everything is connected

In voicework everything is connected. The position of the skeleton determines what the muscles have to do. The muscles control the way we breathe. The way we breathe determines how much air we have available for making sound. A change in one part of the body has a domino effect on the rest. This is something we shall explore in detail in the next chapter. It is, however, important to grasp the concept of centredness or balance from the start.

> *The voice is like a finely-woven tapestry, all threads of the work are interconnected.*
> Patsy Rodenburg

Physical centredness, which frees the body parts to perform the tasks for which they have evolved, is connected to psychological centredness. If we are physically centred, we are more likely to be psychologically alert and calm. This state of relaxed readiness is the ideal for producing a natural, free voice. Clearly our mood state is closely connected to the way we sound. If our mood is off-centre so will our voice be. Think how often your voice has betrayed your mood of irritation, disappointment, boredom, joy, anticipation ...

> *As a barometer of life's pressure, the voice is unfailingly accurate.*
> Patsy Rodenburg

At a different level, our physical and psychological centredness is connected to our spiritual condition. Not everyone will wish to explore this, of course. But if we wish to enter a meditative state, we need to be both physically and psychologically centred.

Because everything is connected, work on your voice will inevitably entail changes elsewhere in your body. Through it you may come to understand better what makes you tick. You may also find the space to understand other unsuspected and unexpected aspects of your makeup.

3 Speaking 'proper' and speaking effectively

This book is not about changing your accent, or offering elocution lessons. It is about helping you to use your voice more effectively.

If your first language is English, you will already have a distinctive accent of some kind. Accents, especially in Britain, are markers of social acceptability or stigma, and many people suffer various forms of discrimination based simply on the accent they use. Some may wish to change their accent to conform to what they perceive as a more acceptable norm. Others may feel a justifiable pride in the badge of identity their accent confers on them. But I shall not focus on these questions in this book. Your accent is your business.

> *All tension comes from anxiety to please, and eventually you have to come round to the view that what you have to offer is good enough.*
> Cicely Berry

Instead, I want you to be able to use your voice more effectively, with less wear and tear, whatever your accent is. If you use your voice more effectively, you will feel greater confidence in it. Confidence in fact tends to override questions of accent. People will listen to you because you sound convincing; they will not be bothered by your accent.

If English is not your first language, you will also have an accent. You may feel that this puts you at a disadvantage compared with 'native speakers'. I do not believe this is true. Your accent is one of the marks of your individuality. And it is not my intention in this book to change your accent into 'Received Pronunciation' (RP). However, I do hope to persuade you that, if you learn to use your voice more effectively, your confidence in your ability to communicate in English will improve dramatically.

4 'It ain't what you do …

… it's the way that you do it,' in the words of the song. No one can do voicework for you. It is something you have to explore yourself. And this implies commitment. When you come to try the exercises later in the book, they will have no effect unless they are done with full physical and mental concentration and commitment. If you simply go through the motions, do not expect much benefit. However, a word of warning – do not approach them as you would an aerobics class. Athleticism is not the aim, rather a relaxed yet focused form of effort. Trying too hard will be counterproductive.

> *I am my own worst enemy; I usually beat myself.*
> Timothy Gallwey

The aims of the book

1 *To raise awareness of the importance of the voice in both professional and personal contexts*

Everything starts with awareness. Until we begin to observe ourselves, we have no chance of understanding how we function, nor of effecting any change. Ironically, it is those things closest to us which are the most difficult to become aware of. To hear yourself as others hear you is literally impossible, but it *is* possible to sharpen considerably your self-perception.

2 *To impart practical skills for developing the voice as a strong and flexible instrument*

A range of exercises and activities will be suggested for improving posture, breathing, phonation, pitch range, articulation and modulation. These begin with relaxation work, which helps to put us into a state of relaxed awareness.

3 *To provide self-help activities for maintaining teachers' voices in good condition*

The care of the voice can be assured by applying some quite simple rules and procedures.

4 *To offer suggested activities for use in class as well as for self-development*

Students can benefit greatly from voicework too, both in terms of enhanced confidence in themselves and increased competence in the language – especially through an understanding of its aesthetic potential.

5 *To offer information on the use of the voice for sustaining physical, psychological and spiritual well-being*

For those who are interested in taking their involvement with voicework further, the book will set out an introduction to the ways in which the voice can create changed mental states and can sustain health, through activities such as toning. This may not be for everybody, but no account of voice would be complete without it.

Who the book is for

Primarily, the book is for any teacher of language. This includes the following categories:

- teachers of English as a foreign or second language, including those for whom English is their first language and those for whom it is a second or foreign language
- teachers of any other language as a foreign or second language, for example teachers of French in the UK, of Spanish in Germany, of Japanese in Singapore, of Mandarin in the USA, etc
- teachers of the first language, for example English teachers in the UK, French teachers in France, Spanish teachers in Argentina, etc

It will also be of interest to teachers of any subject, since all teachers use their voices, whatever they teach. Anyone who needs to use their voice professionally, in whatever capacity, should find this book of use.

The structure of the book

Chapter 1 Developing the voice

Following a section on relaxation techniques, this chapter describes how voice is produced, with activities for developing better posture, breathing, phonation, resonance, articulation and modulation. There are exercises and routines for you to do alone. Some can also be used with the class.

Chapter 2 Voicework in class

This chapter focuses on the integration of voicework in the overall communication process. It offers a range of suggested activities for students in four sections: sensitizing activities; physical warm-ups; work on sounds, words and sentences; working with texts.

Chapter 3 Voice for personal growth

This focuses on how voice can be used to reduce levels of stress, promote better health and open the way for spiritual awareness and growth. A sample of practices will be described.

Chapter 4 Care and maintenance of the voice

This contains a discussion of the factors militating against a well-maintained voice and offers a number of routines and suggestions for voice care. The chapter ends with some suggested workout routines.

Annotated bibliography

This includes brief descriptions/evaluations of the many books relevant to voicework.

List of useful addresses

For those readers who wish to continue to develop their interest in voice.

Alan Maley
December 1999

Chapter 1   # Developing the voice

Introduction

In this chapter I shall suggest some ways of training and developing your voice so that it becomes a more effective instrument of communication. Most of the activities are for your personal use and development, although a few of them could be adapted for use in your class.

In order to effect any lasting improvement in the way you use your voice, you have to want to do it! And you have to realize that it is your own responsibility and that there are no quick or easy fixes. Working on your voice is enjoyable, but it is hard work too. But if there is pain, you will find there is also plenty of gain, as you begin to notice the improvements in your voice quality and control.

Remember too that in voicework, everything is connected. If you are not physically and mentally relaxed, your posture will suffer. If posture is off-centre, your breathing will suffer. If your breathing is shallow or irregular, there will be insufficient air to generate a strong sound. And downstream from a weak sound, features such as resonance, articulation, volume and modulation will also suffer. So although this chapter is divided into separate sections, they are all mutually reinforcing. Work on posture has an effect on breathing. Work on relaxation has an effect on posture, and so on. Nothing is really separate.

> *Sound mind, sound body, sound voice.*
> Stephen Chun Tao Cheng

As you work on your voice, you will gradually become more aware of yourself and your body and how everything works together. Even such apparently mundane activities as eating, sitting down, standing up, walking, lifting things ... all involve complex interactions between muscles. Being mindful of the way you carry out these activities – the way you use yourself – should help you to do it more economically and less damagingly. And this will have an impact on your voice, too. Here again, everything is connected. If you want to find out more about this, the Alexander Technique and the work of Feldenkrais and Rolf are good places to start: see *Books with a focus on physical well-being* in the annotated bibliography.

> *... it is worthwhile to think about what you do with your body before you begin to work on your voice, because for good or ill, that is the foundation upon which your voice use rests.*
> Michael McCallion

The exercises suggested below are clearly only a selection from the wide variety available. You may wish to look at some of the books listed in the annotated bibliography for further ideas.

1 Relaxation

The key to all voicework is to start from a position of minimum tension. In this way, you allow your body to act in the least effortful way. All too often we try to force our bodies to do things rather than allowing them to happen naturally. In this way we get in our own way, rather than trusting that things will happen better if we do not intrude too much in our own process. It's a bit like the centipede, who could walk very well until one day he tried to concentrate on which leg to move first – and couldn't move at all as a result!

a) Semi-supine position

The best position for relaxation, and for many of the other exercises, is the semi-supine. The reason is that when you are lying down, gravity exerts less force on you, so everything you do requires less energy.

You need to find a place to lie down. The floor surface should be carpeted or you should use a thin exercise mat to lie on. A hard surface will damage your back. Put a thin pillow or a book under the back of your head. (You can calculate how thick this should be by standing against a wall with your heels, buttocks and shoulders touching it. Stand normally, not stiffly erect. Then measure the distance between your head and the wall. This is the thickness you will need.)

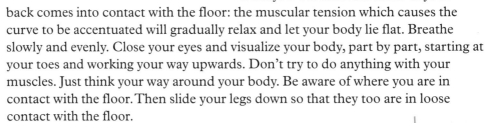

You lie down with knees raised (see diagram), and arms loosely by your side. If you wish, play some soft background music: baroque or New Age is best. Let your body go, do not force it down. Let it find its own contact with the floor. Feel your back spreading on the floor. Don't worry that there is a part of your back which does not touch the floor. This is a natural curvature – and as you do more floor work you will find that more of your back comes into contact with the floor: the muscular tension which causes the curve to be accentuated will gradually relax and let your body lie flat. Breathe slowly and evenly. Close your eyes and visualize your body, part by part, starting at your toes and working your way upwards. Don't try to do anything with your muscles. Just think your way around your body. Be aware of where you are in contact with the floor. Then slide your legs down so that they too are in loose contact with the floor.

This exercise will leave you feeling incredibly relaxed. But apart from that it helps to lengthen the spine and widen the back – both positive effects for your general health and for breathing.

b) Semi-supine plus

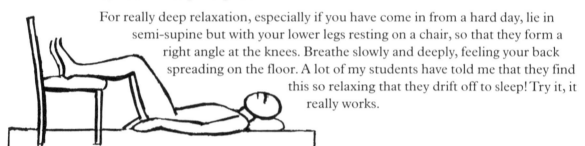

For really deep relaxation, especially if you have come in from a hard day, lie in semi-supine but with your lower legs resting on a chair, so that they form a right angle at the knees. Breathe slowly and deeply, feeling your back spreading on the floor. A lot of my students have told me that they find this so relaxing that they drift off to sleep! Try it, it really works.

Lie in semi-supine (see diagram on p 2) and press different parts of your body towards the floor, one at a time: your heels, your calves, your thighs, your buttocks, the small of your back, the middle back, your shoulders, your neck, your head, your elbows, your wrists, your hands. For each body part, press down for a count of five, then release. Count five before you press down the next part. When you have finished, let yourself melt back into the floor.

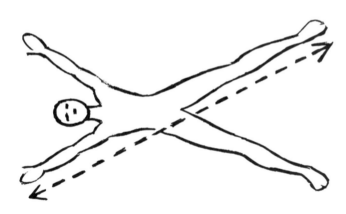

Start in semi-supine. Then stretch out your four limbs in a star-shape. Extend the right arm and left leg as far out as you can. Then relax them. Then do the same with the left arm and the right leg. Do this five times, then go back into relaxed semi-supine.

Start in semi-supine. Tense each part of your body in turn, starting with your toes and moving upwards. Hold each part, tensing for a count of five, then let go completely. Count to five before tensing the next part. Finally, tense the whole of your body, clenching all your muscles at once. Let go on a big sigh, and go back to relaxed semi-supine.

The last three exercises above all involve tensing muscles, then releasing them. It may sound paradoxical but you can't completely relax a muscle until it has been tensed. Try it for yourself: rest your arm on a table normally and try to 'relax' it. It's incredibly difficult because the muscle 'thinks' it is already relaxed. Then try tensing it, and releasing it, and notice the difference.

c) Down on your knees!

Still using a mat or carpet, take up the kneeling position (see diagram on the next page). Your arms should be slightly bent, and so should your legs, so that you are evenly supported, with your back in a straight line. Your head should hang down loosely so that there is no neck tension. Let your belly hang loose!

In this position, take long, even breaths. On each in-breath, raise your head slowly and without strain. Lower it on the out-breath. Take ten breaths like this. Then take another ten breaths. This time rock your body forwards, raising your head on the in-breath, and rock backwards letting your head go down on the out-breath. Feel the breath filling you completely each time.

Because your arms and legs are supporting you, your chest and abdomen are free of tension. This makes it easier simply to breathe relaxation into you.

d) On your feet!

Stand in the balanced position: comfortably erect, eyes straight ahead in a tension-free gaze, shoulders loose, hands hanging loosely by your side, knees slightly flexed, feet shoulder-width apart.

This is the perfectly centred position, where your body is least affected by gravity, and where all your muscles are in a state of relaxed readiness to do whatever is needed.

Breathe deeply and regularly, keeping a steady gaze at a point on the wall in front of you. Close your eyes and visualize all the tension or fatigue draining down your body and into the ground beneath your feet. Really feel it percolating through each part of your body in turn until it has all drained away. Still breathing deeply and slowly, draw energy from the earth back into your feet and feel it rising through you till it reaches the crown of your head. By this time you will be fully energized, alert, yet relaxed.

Some people find it difficult to visualize to begin with but usually it gets easier as they go on. So don't give up if you have this problem. You may find it helps to visualize something more concrete, like a plug hole under each heel. Think of weariness and tension draining away like bath water. In drawing energy in, think of bright orange light which streams up through you and out of you like stars from a firework. Or as one of my students reported, 'I think of my volcano – all the energy goes shooting up like molten lava.'

e) Shoulders and neck

These are the parts of your body which (along with the jaw) concentrate most tension, so they need regular checking. If your shoulders are raised by tension, your neck is constricted and the muscles you need for breathing have their attention diverted.

Stand in the balanced position and lift your shoulders as high as you can. Hold them tense for a count of five, then drop them back into place. Do this five times. (If you work with a partner, ask your partner to stand behind you. Leave your shoulders loose and your partner will lift them up and let them drop. Don't try to 'help' your partner by lifting your own shoulders – let her do it.) After this, do five shoulder rolls from back to front and from front to back.

For the neck, let your head drop gently forward onto your chest. Very slowly and gently turn your head so that you are looking sideways over your left shoulder. Then repeat this for the right side. Do the movement five times. Raise your left shoulder and nudge your head loosely to the right, then raise the right shoulder to meet your head, sending it back to the left. Keep up this rippling motion until you have shaken out the tension from your neck.

2   Posture

Most of us lose the naturally good postural habits we are born with. Everyday body use creates new habits which feel normal but which in fact work against good natural posture. The exercises here help to correct poor body use habits and to restore a well-balanced, centred posture.

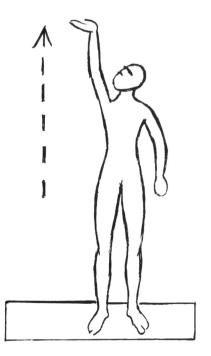

Sleep like a bow.
Stand like a pine.
Sit like a bell.
Walk like the wind.
Tao saying

a) Pushing up the sky

Stand in the balanced position. Extend your right hand and arm above your head with the palm facing upwards. Take a deep breath and release it in one long, smooth out-breath as you push upward in a number of small movements of your arm and hand. Visualize pushing up the sky with your hand. Do this five times then repeat it with the other hand.

b) Unwinding the spine

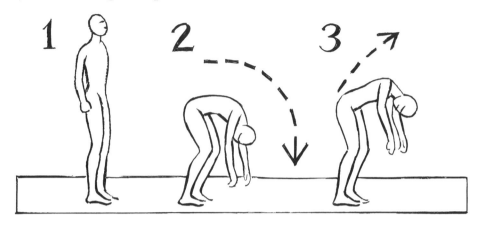

Stand in the balanced position, feet shoulder-width apart. Take a normal breath, then on the out-breath let your body flop forward from the waist, hands hanging loosely down (they should fall just above each foot) and head hanging loose. Take two or three breaths in this position, feeling the air reaching deep inside you, then come up slowly. Try to unwind one vertebra at a time, leaving the seven neck vertebrae till last. Bring your head up slowly and let it settle gently till it is balanced on top of your spinal column.

This is literally 'unwinding', and it's so easy to do. It's not a bad idea to do this between lessons, if you can find a private place! You'll really feel the benefit of it.

c) The monkey

In the monkey position you are crouched down, feet shoulder-width apart, head and spine erect and in alignment, heels flat on the floor, hands touching the ground between your feet.

First go down halfway to the point where your hands can just reach the ground. Then slowly lower your buttocks till they almost touch the ground. Then come up slowly on an in-breath, letting your head lead the movement, as if you were being pulled up by a thread like a puppet. Do this five times.

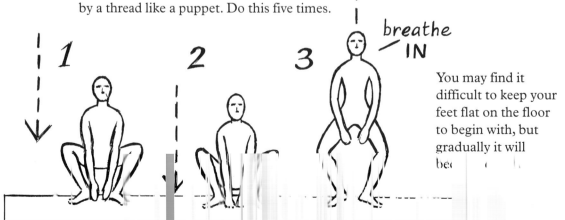

You may find it difficult to keep your feet flat on the floor to begin with, but gradually it will bec

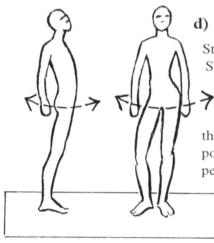

d) Pelvic rocking

Start from the balanced standing position. Slowly rock your pelvic girdle from front to back and back again. Do this a few times rhythmically. Then rock it from side to side by shifting the weight from one hip joint to the other and back. Come back to the balanced position, releasing any tension in your legs. The pelvis will fall back into place.

e) Diving in

breathe
IN

breathe
OUT

1   2   3

Stand as if you were about to launch into a dive: knees slightly bent, arms bent slightly out in front, body slightly inclined to the front. Then, on the in-breath, throw your hands behind you and bend forward, as if you were just about to launch yourself forward. Then on the out-breath return to the starting position. Do this several times. The last time you do it, return slowly to the erect balanced position again.

In both d) and e), you are going out of alignment in order to come back to a better alignment. It's a bit like having to tense muscles before you can release them. By moving away from the point your body 'thinks' is centred, you make it easier to find your natural point of perfect alignment.

3   Breathing

Breathing is the first and last thing we do.
Patsy Rodenburg

Soun is noght but eyr ybroken,
And every speche that ys spoken,
Lowd or pryvee, foul or fair,
In his substaunce ys but air.
Geoffrey Chaucer

a)   Semi-supine

- Lie in semi-supine, with legs drawn up to form a triangle with the floor. Take a breath and as you release it, slowly slide your left leg down till it is flat on the floor. On the in-breath draw it back up again. Do this five times with alternate legs, focusing on where the air is going inside your body. Do not force yourself to breathe deeply, just let it happen, nice and slowly.
- Lying in semi-supine, take a breath, then release it as slowly as you can, making a –*ffffff* sound as you do so. Make the out-breath last longer each time you do it. Then do the same releasing your breath on a long –*aaaaah* sound.

I love making that 'aaaaah' sound. It really makes me feel as if I've emptied out.
(Charlene, voice student)

b)   Hug yourself tight

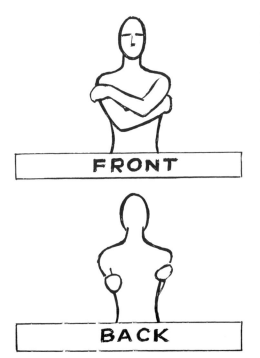

FRONT

BACK

Stand in the balanced, centred position (see p 4). Put your right hand under your left armpit and your left arm around your right upper arm. Hug yourself tight in this position and take several slow, regular breaths, drawing the air in as deep as you can. Then take an in-breath and on the out-breath, let your body fall forward from the waist. Take several breaths while you are down. Feel the air opening up your lower back. Then come up slowly on an in-breath. Repeat the process with your left hand under your right armpit and your right hand round your left upper arm.

It really feels as if the air is pushing right down to the bottom of my back – as if I had lungs right down there. (Jason, student)

c) Conducting the orchestra

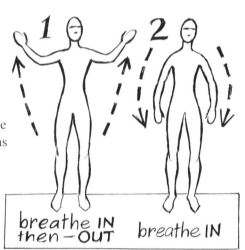

breathe IN then –OUT   breathe IN

Visualize yourself as a famous orchestral conductor. Stand in the balanced position. Breathe in as you raise your arms to shoulder height, slightly towards the front, hands loose. Look to the right and the left, as if at the musicians. Breathe out and relax. Just as you are about to start, someone in the audience drops a bottle. Disgusted, you drop your hands to your sides. At the same time you take in a deep breath of annoyance. Repeat the process three times.

This is based on an idea in Michael McCallion's *The Voice Book* (Faber & Faber 1988).

d) Blowing out candles

Stand in the balanced position. Imagine there are twelve candles in a row in front of you. Take a breath, then blow out the candles one by one. Make sure you have enough breath left for the last one!

Great for breath control. You really have to keep enough air back for the last one. The kids in my class loved it too. (Cheryl, teacher trainee)

e) Flat tyre

Take a full breath from the balanced standing position. Imagine you are a fully inflated car tyre. Suddenly you get a puncture. Let the air out in a slow *–sssss* until the tyre is completely flat. Do this for all four tyres!

Such a lot of fun, this one. I used it with my students too. They loved it. (Daren, teacher trainee)

f) Reverse breathing

The object of this exercise is to develop your awareness of the normal breathing process by experiencing its opposite! Normally you would breathe by pulling air in and pushing down the diaphragm, causing your abdomen to swell. As you breathe out, your abdomen flattens. Take four breaths like this to feel the sensation it gives you. Then try pushing out your chest and pulling in your abdomen on the in-breath; collapse your chest while throwing out your abdomen on the out-breath. Try alternating between the two ways of breathing.

I felt that this gave me a lot more control over all my breathing muscles, though it felt a bit strange at first. (Huang, teacher trainee)

g) **Vacuuming the lungs**

From the balanced standing position, take a deep breath. Then breathe out completely, emptying your lungs. When you are completely empty, close your mouth and pinch your nostrils so that you cannot take in any air. Now expand your ribcage and abdomen as if you were breathing – but do not take in any air, just move the muscles. When you are at maximum expansion, let go of your nostrils. There will be a sudden rush of air into your lungs. A great clean-out! Also a way of getting your breathing muscles to work without actually breathing, so that you can feel what actually happens when you really do breathe.

This idea comes from Kristin Linklater's *Freeing the Natural Voice* (Drama Book Publishers 1976).

I think this was the first time I realized how many muscles were involved in the simple act of breathing. It sort of cleans you out too … (Clarinda, voice student)

4   **Onset of the voice/resonance**

The voice is produced when air vibrates the vocal cords (actually a couple of flaps of flesh across the larynx). But the sound we produce would be very small if it were not amplified by our resonators. Resonators are simply cavities in our bodies whose shape helps to give sounds their typical colour. Just as a violin is a hollow box which resonates to produce a sound typical of the violin, so do our chests, throats, mouths, noses, sinuses and cranial bones resonate to produce the particular combination of pitches which make each of our voices so distinctive. The aim of the following activities is to get the sound moving smoothly and to experiment with different resonators.

a) **Semi-supine**

Lying relaxed in semi-supine, let your breath out as a long sigh. Do this several times. Sound the note –*aaaaah* on the out-breath. Make it last as long as your breath lasts. Try making it last longer. Feel the vibrations in your body as you do it. Where do you feel them most? Spend some time tuning in to the vibrations. Make the sound –*oooooh* as low in your voice as you can. Put your hand on your chest and feel it rumbling. Then make the same sound come from your mouth and face area. Put your hands lightly on your cheeks and jaw and feel the vibrations. Then make the sound come from the top of your head. Put your fingers lightly on your forehead and scalp and feel the vibrations.

I was amazed that even my forehead was vibrating – and the top of my head too. (Kevin, voice student)

Do the same series of notes using different sounds: –*eeeeee*, –*aaaaah*, –*oooooor*, –*errrrr*, –*aiiiii*, –*auuuu*.

What I enjoyed most was just playing around with the sounds and working out which bits of me were vibrating as I shifted up and down. (Sunil, voice student)

b) Hum into your palms

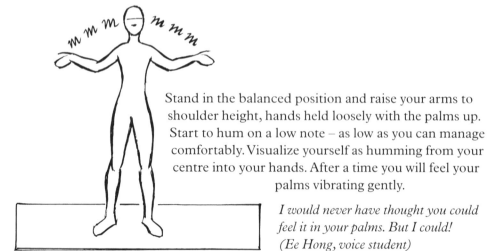

Stand in the balanced position and raise your arms to shoulder height, hands held loosely with the palms up. Start to hum on a low note – as low as you can manage comfortably. Visualize yourself as humming from your centre into your hands. After a time you will feel your palms vibrating gently.

I would never have thought you could feel it in your palms. But I could!
(Ee Hong, voice student)

c) The touch of sound

From a standing position, flop over at the waist. As you come up, unwinding the vertebrae, take a breath so that you are full by the time you are erect. Then release a touch of sound: *–huh.* Then again: *–huh.* Go on doing this till you have no more air left. Then start again. Visualize the note bouncing off your diaphragm, as if it were a trampoline. Put your hand lightly on your middle as you do this and feel the bouncing movement of the muscles. Then repeat the process in semi-supine.

d) Mouth and nose

Keeping your lips lightly closed, hum vigorously until you feel your lips vibrating – it may even tickle a bit. Then experiment with adding a vowel sound to the *–mmmmm*: *–mmmmmah, –mmmmmoo, –mmmmmii, –mmmmmey.*

Then repeat the process making a *–nnnnnn* sound. Feel the vibrations in your nose. Add vowel sounds as before. Notice the way the vibrations in your nose on the *–nnnnn* combine with those that come through your mouth on the vowels. Then repeat the process with *–nnnggg* and with the vowels. Feel the release of your soft palate when the vowel pops out.

I tried to imagine I was an African pronouncing the place name 'Ngorongoro'.
(Steven, voice student)

> *Don't be afraid to play with the voice. Step outside the narrow tracks of your ordinary voice use as a regular part of your training.*
> Michael McCallion

e) Sliding and gliding

Try these exercises for exploring and extending your vocal range.

- Do a 'miaow' like a cat, starting as high in your voice as you can and sweeping down to your lowest note. Do it as slowly as you can, using up all the breath. Keep doing it until you have a smooth curve of sound, without any blips.

- Imitate a police siren: *–eeeeee/–oooooo* (repeated). The *–eeeeee* should be at the top of your voice and the *–oooooo* right at the bottom.
- Imagine you are on one side of a valley and your friend is on the other. Greet her with *Hi!* starting really high and swooping down through your vocal range.
- Standing in the balanced position, let go on the sound *–aaaaah*, starting at your highest note and moving smoothly down to your lowest growl. You may find that at one point there is a sudden pitch break. Work to eliminate this so that your voice moves seamlessly down through the curve. Then reverse the process, moving up from the bottom to the top note. You may find it useful to visualize your voice as a lift moving from the basement to the top storey. This is a useful exercise to do just before you have to give a public presentation. If you do it quickly a couple of times, then speak a sentence with your normal voice, you will find that your voice has a more comfortable pitch. This is your real voice, not the one you often strain to produce.

f)   A smooth getaway

Some people have difficulty with words beginning with vowels. They produce a hard glottal attack rather than a smooth sound at the front of the mouth. If you have this problem, try putting a silent *h* in front of the vowel. Breathe the sound out. *h … attack*, *h … infantry*, *h … exercise*, etc. After a time, a smooth onset will become habitual.

5   Articulation

Articulation refers to the way we chop up the sound after it comes through the vocal cords, using the teeth, the tongue, the soft palate and the jaw. There are two basic kinds of exercise for articulation: for warming up the articulators, and for practising particular sounds.

a)   Warming up the articulators

Face muscles

Play with your facial muscles: raise one eyebrow, then the other; flare one nostril, then the other; wrinkle your nose up as high as possible; clench your whole face as tightly as you can; pull your cheeks sideways in an exaggerated grimace; tense the tendons that connect your chin to your throat; stretch your face laterally – from the right eye to the left side of your mouth, then from top right to bottom left.

I felt like a real idiot at first! Then I realized just how many muscles there are in the face, and how hard it is to isolate them. I still have trouble raising my right eyebrow without pulling up the left one with it! But I'm working on it! (Wendy, voice student)

Jaws

Make a circular chewing movement to the right, then to the left. Ta
jaw lightly between the finger and thumb of each hand. Let the jaw
your muscles from holding it up. Slowly and gently raise and drop
your hands.

It makes you realize just how habitual it is for us to pull up the bottom jaw.
Really difficult to let it go completely. (Sandra, voice student)

Gently massage the jaw joint (on a level with your ears) with a circular movement.

Lips

Alternately pout your lips forward, then spread them wide. Draw your lips into your mouth so that they cover your teeth. Then pop them out as you release the air in your mouth. Make a *–brrrrr* sound by expelling air through your lips to make them vibrate. Try doing it on a *–prrrrr* without voicing.

Tongue

Stick your tongue as far out as you can. Then curl the tip backwards as far as you can till it touches your soft palate. Do this five times. Place the tip of your tongue against your bottom teeth. Keep it rooted there as you alternately make the sounds *–aaaaah* and *–eeeeee*. Notice the way your tongue changes shape as you do this. With the tongue rooted against your bottom teeth again, push the middle of your tongue as far forward out of your mouth as possible. Then pull it back in as far as you can. Repeat the complete movement five times.

It's disgusting! But I'd never realized just what a big muscle my tongue was!
(Anjali, voice student)

Soft palate and throat aperture

Do a big yawn. Notice how big your throat opening becomes. Use a mirror to observe yourself. Release the air in your throat by flapping open your soft palate in a *–khaaaa* sound. Do this several times and visualize the small explosion at the back of your mouth. Then reverse the direction of the air and suck it in, again feeling the explosion as it breaks through in a *–khaaaa*. Do the movement in both directions alternately ten times. Then try to do it without actually yawning, keeping your mouth closed. Think of it as a suppressed yawn.

I never realized how enormous my throat hole was! You could pour a bucket of coal down
it! (Peter, voice student)

b) Practising particular sounds

There may well be sounds you have problems with in English. This is certainly the case for non-native speakers of English but native speakers often experience difficulties too. There is no space here to give full examples of the sorts of practice sentences or texts you can try. However, there are many good practice paragraphs in Michael McCallion's *The Voice Book* pp 146–72, and in Malcolm Morrison's *Clear Speech* (see annotated bibliography).

The kinds of sounds you may have problems with are the w/v distinction and the r/l distinction. These can be tackled by practising sentences like these:

Winsome Vera lived a long life in Windsor with Vincent and went to work in
Vernon's in the West End.

Red lemons are rarely left ripening on the red lemon trees because when they
ripen a lot, they rot.

6 Modulation

Here we are concerned with giving an affective tone to the voice. There is really no substitute here for reading a text aloud and experimenting with different moods and intentions. Begin with sentences (see Chapter 2 for some examples). Notice how the same string of words can be given completely different meanings depending on how they are spoken. Try saying *I had a great day today* as if you really meant it, and then as if it were a bitter statement about your wholly unsuccessful day.

a) Chunking and mood swings

Take a fairly short text (the Polish textbook writer Leszek Szkutnik has some wonderful short texts in his *Lyrics in English*). Decide how you are going to read it – where you will need to pause for the sense to come through, where to pause for effect, what mood you want to convey – joy, anger, disappointment, uncertainty, etc; who you are talking to, and so on. Then try it. But then try it again with a different mood and intention. It is best if you work with a partner but you can also do it by recording yourself on an audio or video tape. Here is an example from Szkutnik's *Lyrics in English*:

They are good people. Almost all of them. They may not see you. They may not help you. They may not understand you. But they are good. They mean well.

b) Semi-supine speaking

Try speaking a short text aloud while lying in semi-supine. You will need to commit it to memory, not read it from a script. For example:

Everyone knows about it. But no one says anything. How can we go on like this when no one even admits there is a problem? Yes, a problem. You mean you haven't noticed anything either? Not even you? Then I think the world really has gone crazy. Who else can I turn to, if not you?

Remember to relax completely and to take advantage of the fact that you don't have to fight gravity. Your voice should come out effortlessly. Then try speaking it with different moods, intentions, emphases. Record yourself if you can and listen critically afterwards. Listen to yourself as if you were someone else.

7 Volume

Whenever I talk to people about voicework, they almost always say, 'Ah, yes, voice projection ...' and of course, it is true that we need to make sure that our voices match the size of the space they are working in. But there is no magic formula for projecting your voice. Most of the work you need to do is

a) Sweet and low

When you next have a class, begin by speaking very softly. You may even begin by moving your lips but not vocalizing. When you speak softly, the audience tends to listen harder, in case they miss something. You will be surprised at how far your voice carries when people are listening to what you say!

When I tried this, I was amazed at the effect it had. Gradually they noticed I was moving my lips but they couldn't hear anything. One by one, they fell silent. As they did, I gradually increased my volume to normal. (Prakash, teacher trainee)

b) Off the wall

Decide on a sentence to speak. Stand about a yard from a wall and speak it. Then move back another yard and speak it again. Keep doing this until you are a long way from the wall. You have to match your voice to the distance from the wall. The farther away you are, the more effort you have to make to reach it with your voice.

c) The fishing line

Stand at the front of the space you will have to speak in. Then, as you begin to speak, make the motion with your right arm of someone casting a fishing line towards the back of the space. Visualize your voice snaking out with the fishing line, in a great curve which reaches the back of the space. Alternatively, think of your voice as an arrow which you shoot in a long, smooth arc towards the back of the space. See its trajectory in your mind's eye.

d) Crescendo

Start to speak your lines or text very softly. Gradually increase the volume to the point just before a shout. Then go back down again.

e) Radio tuning

Imagine that you are tuning a radio set. Decide on a text to read (it might be a newscast), then read it through the changes of intensity on the different wave bands. Your voice should go louder and softer as you pass through the wave bands.

I had a lot of fun with this one. I tried it with my class too. They were better than me at the sound effects. (Cheryl, teacher trainee)

Concluding remarks

If you do at least some of the above exercises on a regular basis, your voice quality, range and expressivity will almost certainly improve.

> *It's not that I don't know what to do, it's that I don't do what I know.*
> Timothy Gallwey

Chapter 2   # Voicework in class

Introduction

In Chapter 1 the focus was on the personal benefits you can derive from voicework as a teacher, in terms of greater awareness, greater control and greater confidence in your ability to use your voice in a variety of ways. The way your own voice quality affects the classroom atmosphere, the relationships you have with the students, the energy and enjoyment they derive from the way you use your voice, will all be obvious to you. But there is every reason to incorporate voicework into your normal classroom activities with students too, so that they can share in some of these benefits.

The principal advantages of incorporating voicework in classes are:

- Students generally come to feel more relaxed about their language learning.
- Their energy levels improve dramatically.
- Their motivation improves, and their general attitude towards learning the language becomes more positive.
- Many of the activities offered here also have a direct language-learning payoff, in addition to any psychological and physical benefits they may have.
- Using voicework on a regular basis with your students gives you the incentive to continue working on your own voice!

However, before you start to introduce voicework to your students, it will be advisable to take them into your confidence by explaining the advantages of this kind of work to them. Help them to understand how crucial our voices are in conducting our lives, how much more alive we can feel by working on our voices, and how voicework can contribute significantly to their progress and confidence in the foreign language (as well as in their mother tongue). Reassure them that everything they will be asked to do has a purpose, and that none of it is threatening. In fact, it will make their classes more enjoyable.

For convenience, this chapter is divided into the four parts listed above. You should note that this is not an ordered sequence. It would be sensible to do some sensitizing activities towards the beginning of your programme, but after that there is no necessary order. It is also desirable to start every class with some physical warm-up or relaxation activities. You will be the best judge of when it is appropriate to introduce a particular activity.

1   Sensitizing activities

Most students are likely to be just as unaware of the nature and characteristics of the human voice as are most teachers. They will therefore need to start noticing things about their own and others' voices, and to realize how important voices are as a badge of identity and as an instrument of self-expression.

The following is a representative set of awareness-raising activities.

a)   A world of sound

> *Not knowing how to listen, neither can they speak.*
> Heraclitus

Careful listening is an important component of voicework, and this activity is a first step in becoming more aware of the world of sound. You might also like to use it as an introduction to a listening comprehension lesson, just to help students to 'tune in'.

- Ask students to close their eyes and listen intently to all the sounds around them for three minutes. They then discuss with you what they heard.
- Students repeat the activity but this time they listen to sounds within themselves.

The most likely sound they will mention is their breathing. Other possibilities include the sounds of their heartbeat pulsing in their ears, joints creaking or cracking, tummy rumbling ...

When I tried this myself, I found I could hear my breathing quite easily, but it was some time before I could really hear my heartbeat. What I didn't notice at first was my own silent, yet 'noisy' monologue, which got in the way of my concentration on the 'real' sounds in me. I began to realize that this also gets in the way when we listen – or rather, don't listen – to other people too. (Françoise, teacher trainee)

It may be worth exploring with the students this 'interior monologue' through which they verbalize their thoughts and feelings. The 'noise' of this monologue is what often prevents us from listening to what others are saying, or even from speaking clearly what we ourselves really want to say. One of the functions of the relaxation exercises is to still this babble of internal voices. When we've done that, we're usually in a much more alert state.

We are surrounded by sound (and noise!). Many sounds are taken so much for granted that we no longer notice them (eg the hum of strip-lighting, fans, air-conditioners, etc). Yet some sounds can bring us great pleasure, if we take the trouble to notice them (see Mathieu's *The Listening Book* in the annotated bibliography). Other sounds are actually dangerous to our health – noise pollution is an ever-present danger – and it is important to be aware of this.

b) Listening to singing

Many students listen to a rather narrow range of vocal styles. The object of this activity is simply to expose them to the sheer variety of effects which the human voice can achieve. You may like to make listening to new kinds of vocal styles a regular part of most lessons. I very often play a new kind of singing as students come into the class, partly to arouse their curiosity, partly to extend their experience of the human voice and partly to set the atmosphere.

Play extracts from a variety of singing styles, for example classical north Indian, Russian Orthodox church choirs, Tibetan chanting, flamenco, Gregorian chanting, Schubert Lieder, soul, blues, spirituals, grand opera, Bulgarian polyphonic choirs, Lisboan fado, Swiss yodelling, classical Arabic, Jewish cantors, Chinese opera, Japanese shigin, Vedic chanting, etc. Ask the students to decide which extracts they prefer, then discuss their choices. What is it about their chosen style which makes it special? How does it make them feel? You may need to supply some vocabulary here – *high/low pitch, melody, harmony, tenor, bass*, etc.

The search for different types of singing and other uses of the voice is fascinating in itself, and I have discovered so many styles I had never suspected the existence of. I have also found that students, once their interest is aroused, will bring in lots of new and interesting samples. You may want to set up a project to develop a sound archive. This can lead into oral presentations by students, introducing particular styles or singers, writing catalogue entries and reviews, designing brochures and much more.

When I asked each nationality in my class to present a singer from their own country, I had not anticipated the response! Not only was the stuff they brought in really interesting to listen to, but the discussion was so animated, I couldn't stop them from talking! (Mike, teacher trainee)

c) Me and my voice

It comes as a surprise to most of us when we hear our own recorded voice for the first time. ('Is that really me? I can't believe I sound like that.') Generally we are very unaware of what we sound like to others – and even a tape recording cannot tell us that. And most of the time, we don't think about how our voice sounds at different times and in different contexts. The aim of this activity is to raise awareness of these factors.

Ask students to complete the questionnaire on p 19 and then discuss their answers in groups of three before reporting back to the whole class.

When I thought about the questions before class, the thing that struck me most was the way I change my voice when I speak English. I think it's got something to do with the shape your mouth has to be in for speaking English. I also rec

MY VOICE

1 How many different ways have I listened to my own voice?
- On a tape recording? ☐
- On a video film? ☐
- In my own head as I speak? ☐
- On my answering machine? ☐
- As an echo in the mountains? ☐
- Any others? _____

2 Am I a fast or slow speaker of my own language?

_____

3 When do I speak faster? And when slower?

_____

4 Am I a faster or slower speaker than others in my family?

_____

5 Do I tend to speak loudly or softly?

_____

6 When do I speak more loudly or softly?

_____

7 When I speak in English do I change the speed, or the loudness?

_____

8 What is different about my voice when I speak in English?

_____

9 Does my voice change when I speak on the phone? If so, how?

_____

10 Is my voice different at different times of the day?
(eg first thing in the morning or late at night)

_____

11 Has anyone ever commented on the way my voice sounds to them?
What did they say?

_____

12 Who is my favourite voice? (actor, singer, friend ...)
What is it that makes their voice so attractive to me?

_____

Adapted from a
questionnaire
designed by
Mario Rinvolucri.

One of the things that often dawns on students as a result of this activity is that they can change the way they sound. Sometimes it is worth pointing out the way actors change their voices for different roles. Meryl Streep and Marlon Brando are good examples. Other actors make a 'trade mark' of their vocal style – for example, Sylvester Stallone or Hugh Grant.

d) The tell-tale voice

The fact that we ARE our voices, that they are an integral and intimate part of our personalities, was discussed in Chapter 1. Every time we hear a stranger speak, we make judgements about his or her personality. This activity aims to help raise students' sensitivity to voice factors such as pitch, loudness and texture in making these personality judgements.

For this activity you need a two-minute clip from a film which is not in English. You also need an audio tape on which you have recorded brief extracts of about ten people speaking in English. These people's voices should be as varied as possible. (One good source of such voices are the recorded dialogues from published course materials.)

- Tell the students about the clip they are to watch. As they watch, they make notes about the personalities, ages and appearance of the characters. Let them compare notes after the viewing.

- Now tell them that they are to choose some English actors to dub the film into English. Play them the selection of male and female voices on the audio tape. In pairs, they decide which English voices would be suitable for each role. Pairs then try to reach agreement in class discussion.

The first time I tried this, there was remarkable agreement about which voices fitted which personalities but there was a lot of discussion about why. In another class there was a lot of disagreement about the allocation of voices to characters. But in both classes, there was no shortage of interesting things to say. (Brenda, teacher)

This activity is based on one in *Listening* by Goodith White in the Oxford Resource Books for Teachers series.

As a follow-up, you could ask students to think of one person whose voice they particularly like, and one whose voice they hate. Perhaps a teacher they had in the past (!) What is it about the voices which give them these feelings?

e) The voice I like best

This activity again helps to raise awareness of different voice qualities and their effects on listeners. You will need to make an audio tape of up to ten different English voices. Preferably they should all speak the same text, lasting not more than one or two minutes.

Play the voices one at a time, with pauses between them. Students make notes on each voice they hear. Then, in groups of four, they rank the voices: which one was most attractive? In discussion they justify their choices.

As a follow-up, students can be asked to prepare to read a short passage in three different voices (these might be deep and chesty, high pitched and squeaky, plus their normal speaking voice). In groups of four, students read in the three different styles. The others ___ ___ which of the three voice they ___ ___ for ___ group members. The foll ___-up encourages students to ___ ___ ___ 'playing around' with ___ ___ voices. It may even help them ___ ___ ___ characteristically ___ ___ ___ voice.

When I designed ___ ___ y, I had adolescent and adult l ___ ___ ___s ___ ___ as thought about it, I ___ liz ___ hat this is great for young lear ___ ___ oo li ___ ___ a ___ not fully articulate about why they prefer a given voice, they usually have very strong opinions. You might like to structure the activity for them by getting them to tick emoticons: ☺ or ☹. Young learners also love the follow-up where they have to imitate different voices. You can add spice to this by asking them to play the parts of Father Bear, Mother Bear and Baby Bear in the Goldilocks story: 'Who's been eating my porridge?'

f) How do they sound?

We constantly make judgements about other people's personality, background, age, mood and intentions on the basis of the way their voices sound. This activity aims to make them more aware of the kinds of judgements we make.

Make an audio recording of up to ten voices speaking in English. They should be as varied as possible (eg male/female, old/young, from different social backgrounds, high/low pitch, expressing different moods, etc). The extracts should last about a minute. You can include voices of famous people recorded off air as well as 'ordinary' speakers of English.

Students are then given the scale below. As they listen, they mark the point on each scale which they think fits the speaker. Then, in pairs, students compare their judgements as a preparation for class discussion.

OLD	< .... >	YOUNG
EDUCATED	< .... >	UNEDUCATED
FRIENDLY	< .... >	UNFRIENDLY
KIND	< .... >	UNKIND
INTERESTING	< .... >	BORING
INTELLIGENT	< .... >	STUPID
OPTIMISTIC	< .... >	PESSIMISTIC
CONFIDENT	< .... >	NERVOUS
HAPPY	< .... >	SAD
CALM	< .... >	ANGRY
TIRED	< .... >	ENERGETIC

Make sure that the discussion touches on the features of the voices which led them to make their decisions.

As a follow-up, ask students to match a series of pictures of different people with a series of recordings of their voices. Students decide which of the voices would be most likely to:

- lend them some money if they were in need
- interrupt them while they were talking
- order them about
- tell them a funny (or dirty) joke
- be the person who reads the weather forecast

This activity is slightly adapted from one in Dalton and Seidlhofer's *Pronunciation* (OUP 1994).

One of the bits of spin-off learning I noted was vocabulary. The pairs of adjectives got them thinking about other vocabulary items which could have been used, like COLD/WARM, STRONG/WEAK. It was very productive. (Elyane, teacher)

g) Shadowing

The aim of this activity is to help students pay conscious attention to what they hear, and subsequently speak. All too often repetition is mindless; here it is mindful, helping the students to shape and polish what they say before they say it.

Take a very short, simple text. For example:

My Nose

It doesn't breathe;
It doesn't smell;
It doesn't feel
So very well.
I am discouraged
With my nose;
The only thing it
Does is blows.

Dorothy Aldis

Read the text aloud to the students, line by line. They repeat each line after you, trying to reproduce the way you read it as accurately as possible. Do this twice. Then read it again, pausing after each line. This time students repeat after you, but silently: they simply re-hear/rehearse the lines in their mind. Then read it one more time. This time the students shadow you subvocally: that is, they make the movements of their speech organs but do not make any sound. Finally, they whisper the lines after you.

As a follow-up, students work in pairs. Student A reads a short text line by line. Student B shadows her as in the procedure described above. The students then change places.

When I first encountered this technique, I thought it was just the old 'repeat after me' routine. But it really isn't. In this activity, students need to concentrate closely on *noticing*, paying attention to the words and to the vocal quality of the other person. In a sense they enter the sound world of the other person.

One way of extending the activity is to ask students to delay repeating what they hear. You speak a line or a sentence, they take it in and 'hold it' till you tell them to speak it aloud. This leads to even more careful internal rehearsal.

This activity is based on a workshop run by Tim Murphey, Nanzan University, at the LIOJ Seminar, Odawara, Japan in August 1999.

h) The inner workbench

This takes the idea of 'mindful' processing one step further. All too often we rush into speech without reflection. We are in a hurry to hear the result. In this activity, students are shown how to pay attention to what happens *before* they speak – to the preparation, to the resulting speech. This really pays dividends when they do come to speak.

The teacher says the English sound once only. Students listen to it very carefully with their inner ear. That is, they re-hear it in their mind's ear. Then they say it in the mind's voice. That is, they rehearse it in their mind only. This is not subvocalization, for there is no movement of speech organs. Then they move almost to the point of saying it, without moving the speech organs. Then they whisper it. Then they speak it – but softly. Finally, they voice it fully.

After this, reverse the process, moving progressively back to the sound in the inner ear. Next, students go through the same process – but this time they change what they repeat from the teacher's voice to their own voice.

The same process can be done with words, with phrases, with whole sentences. These exercises require enormous concentration, yet are extremely powerful in making students aware of their own inner process.

> *The idea of the inner workbench is to provide access to the 'before muscles'*
> *component, to the subtle inner thought or movement before amplification, so that*
> *we can approach learning from two ends not just one.*
> Adrian Underhill

In other words, we are trying to help students understand what they do *before* they speak, not simply to assess what they say and how they say it. A simple demonstration of this is to ask students to get ready to say a phrase (eg *What's the time?*) but then to stop themselves from saying it just before the speech organs start to move. What do they notice about the muscular tension in the speech organs?

I learnt this technique from Adrian Underhill in Barcelona in 1999.

Obviously there is enormous potential here for pronunciation teaching. Activities like this can become a regular part of any lesson, focusing on sounds or words you want to teach. When I tried this on myself, I found it very difficult to separate off the inner ear from the mind's voice. But as I persisted, I found I could give each of them a 'location' inside my head, so that gradually I could distinguish each of them more clearly from each other. See how it works for you before you try it with your students.

2 Physical warm-up activities: relaxation and breathing

It may be useful, before you start to introduce this kind of work in the classroom, to explain why it is beneficial. No athlete would pitch straight into her sport without warming up first. Actors and singers spend a lot of time on warming up their bodies and voices before performing. Because the voice is both psychological (the impulse to speak starts in the brain) and physical, it makes sense to get into the right frame of mind before you start, and to make sure your body is ready too. This is particularly the case in schools or colleges where the students move from one lesson to the next without much of a break in between.

These relaxation and warm-up activities, though short, help to make a clean break between what has gone before (maths or history, perhaps) and what is to come – English. They set up a new, energized atmosphere in the group. And once the students become accustomed to them, they come to form part of an expected routine.

Many of these activities also provide opportunities for enjoyable language learning. Of course, young learners in particular will enjoy the physical activity they offer. But do not underestimate the value of physical involvement for learners of all ages. I currently teach a class of MA students in Thailand. Classes run from 7 pm to 9.30 pm. We have regular breaks for 'stretching' and moving. The change in levels of attention this brings about is remarkable (and indispensable!).

Remember, too, to engage the students in discussion of their reactions to any exercise they do. What did they notice? How did it feel? Which exercise did they prefer? This is important, partly because it ensures that they do reflect on what they have done. It also provides additional opportunities for language practice through talking about something 'real' – themselves.

The activities suggested below are only a small selection from the many you might use. I have been mindful that, in most classrooms, students cannot lie on the floor. So these exercises can all be done from a sitting or standing position and do not require vast amounts of space. (If you are fortunate enough to have a studio or hall to work in, however, you might try adapting some of the semi-supine activities from Chapter 1.) Remember that these are only introductory activities, so they should not go on for too long. However, try to make them a regular part of your teaching routine.

a) In the mood

Students sit quietly, preferably with eyes closed, while you play relaxing music for about five minutes. It is important to choose music which is calming. Students should simply be told to listen, become aware of their own breathing and to let their thoughts flow with the music. Possible selections of music might include Hari Prasad Chowrasia Indian flute music; Gregorian chants; Mozart C major piano concerto (Elvira Madigan); almost anything by Albinoni, Vivaldi, Bach or Handel; Eric Satie (Gymnopédies); Kitaro (Silk Road); Debussy (l'Après-midi d'un Faune); Jonathan Goldman (Dolphin Dreams); Don Campbell (Runes); Yanni (Keys to Imagination); or almost any New Age music. See the list of useful addresses for some of the companies distributing suitable music.

b) Guided relaxation 1

Students should be sitting comfortably, backs touching the chair, legs at a relaxed angle, feet on the floor, hands on thighs, head tilted slightly forward, eyes closed. It is important that they keep their eyes closed and try to visualize each part of the body as it is mentioned. You then speak the following in a calm, rhythmical voice, pausing between each utterance to leave time for the students to feel the full weight of the words. You may like to play some calming music very softly as background.

I feel calm, relaxed, at peace. (repeat)
I can feel the contact of my feet with the floor
My feet are in con...
I can feel my legs...
My ... and my b...
I can feel my back...
I can feel my han...
My ... ds and a...

This sequence
has been slightly
adapted from
Bernard Dufeu's
Teaching Myself
(OUP 1994).

I can feel my head in contact with my neck. (repeat)
My whole body is in contact with the floor and the chair. (repeat)
I feel calm, relaxed, at peace.

When you have finished, ask students to open their eyes. Give them a moment or two to 'come back', and perhaps to stretch their arms and legs.

c) Guided relaxation 2

Students sit in a relaxed way as in the previous activity. Use background music if you wish. Tell them that you are going to talk them through their bodies from toes to head. As you mention each part, they should try to send their minds to that part and visualize it – from outside and from inside.

Feel your toes. Try to feel each one separately.
Now feel your feet – the soles of your feet, your heels …
Send your mind into your ankles. Let them relax.
Now move to your calves. Let go of tension. See them in your mind.
Move to your knees. Let them relax. Smooth the tension away with your mind.
Now relax your thighs. Feel their weight. Let go of tension. Relax.

You continue, talking them through their buttocks, the small of the back, the back, the shoulders, the chest, the neck, the upper and lower arms, the wrists, the hands, the fingers, the cheeks, the jaw, the forehead, the scalp. When you have finished, ask them to visualize the return pathway to the toes, passing through each body part separately. Then let them 'come back' slowly and stretch if they feel like it.

d) Guided relaxation 3

This is best done with students standing up. As you mention each part of the body, they tense it as tightly as they can. When you say *Relax*, they release the tension.

Tense your toes. Hold it … Tighter, tighter … Now let go.
Clench your whole foot, like a fist. Hold it … Tighter … Now let go.
Now tense your calf muscles … Keep them tightly tensed … Tighter … Now let go.

Continue with thighs, buttocks, abdomen, chest, shoulders, upper arms, lower arms, fingers, whole hands, neck, whole face.

Now tense your whole body. Tighter … Tighter still … Now let go.

These guided relaxations are remarkably effective. Apart from relaxing the muscles and the mind, they also slow the rate of breathing. And they are excellent in language-teaching terms for revising the parts of the body!

e) Letting your body breathe you

Just breathe

Students stand in the balanced position (see p 4). Tell them to put their hands on the bottom of their ribcage (fingers to the front, thumb to the rear) and to breathe deeply. If they are breathing deeply using the whole of their rib cage and pushing the diaphragm down, their hands should feel an outward movement all round from front to back. If their breathing is shallow, their hands will only go up and down. When they have got used to the sensation, ask them to breathe as deeply as they can as you count to five, then to hold it for a count of five. Then release slowly on a count of ten. It is important for them to become aware of how their breathing works, and to move in the direction of deeper breathing. Without air you cannot make sound!

Hands up!

In the balanced standing position, students raise their arms above their heads as high as possible, bringing their palms together. With hands in this position, they take three deep breaths and release slowly each time. They then come back to the normal standing position and take another three breaths.

This exercise helps to open the ribcage and the muscles below it on each side of the body. When students take breaths in the normal position after doing it, they will find their breathing is deeper and easier.

Leaning over sideways

Students stand in the balanced position and put their hands behind their heads, linking their fingers. They then lean as far as possible to the right, keeping the body in alignment. In this position they take and release three breaths. They repeat the action on the left side. This again serves to open up the ribcage and the lateral muscles controlling breathing.

Handcuffed

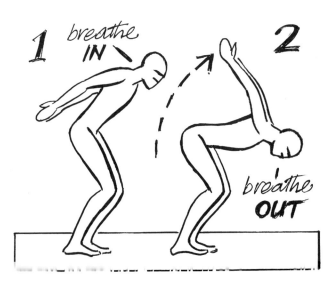

Starting from the balanced standing position, students link their hands behind their backs, turning the palms outwards, and keeping them about 20 cm away from their backs. In this position they take a deep breath. They then bend forward from the waist, raising their linked hands as high as possible. Then breathe out. They repeat this three times. This again opens up the back muscles which control breathing.

The owl

In the balanced standing position, students place their right hand on the area between the neck and the left shoulder. They then breathe in as they swivel their head to look to the right and pull back both shoulders. Eyes should be kept on the same level throughout the movement. They return their head to centre on the out-breath, then turn it towards the other shoulder on the in-breath again, pulling both shoulders back. They repeat the movement three times. They then change hands,

placing the left hand on the right side, and repeat the actions. You can also add sound to the out-breath *–whoooo*, like an owl. Young learners love this one.

The action of pulling back the shoulders opens the ribcage and helps them to push the diaphragm down further.

This idea comes from Chris Brewer and Don Campbell's *Rhythms of Learning* (Zephyr Press 1991).

f) Shake it all about

Starting from the balanced standing position, students shake their hands loosely, arms down. They then shake their legs, without taking feet off the ground. Finally they do a complete body shakeout. They repeat the shakeout, keeping a smile on their faces. Then they do it with a 'blither' – blowing air through their lips (as if imitating a motorbike). Finally they do it taking a deep breath first, then shouting *Hi!* as they shake it all out. A great way of literally shaking the tension out of your body. Young learners especially enjoy this one.

g) Oiling the parts

These are brief warm-up exercises for the speech organs. They are always fun to do and are a very effective way to loosen up the organs of speech. They are a great way to start a lesson, especially with young learners.

Yawn

Ask students to yawn a big yawn. What do they notice about the back of their throats when they yawn? Then ask them to yawn keeping their mouth closed. Can they feel the back of the throat opening wide? Tell them to do it again at home, using a mirror to observe the back of their throats opening. It's dramatic!

Tongue

Ask them to push out their tongues as far as they can, really stretching them. Then to curl the tip of the tongue as far back in the mouth as possible, till it touches the soft palate (or even the uvula). They then alternate the two movements – pushing out and curling back – five times.

Lips

Ask them to push their lips as far forward as possible in an exaggerated pout. Then to spread their lips sideways as far as possible. Again, alternate the two movements five times.

Soft palate

Get them to make the sound –*kaaaah* on the out-breath. Can they feel the pop of air as the soft palate flips upwards to release the air? Then get them to make the same sound on the in-breath. Alternate the two movements five times.

h) The trumpet

Explain that the throat is like a tube or pipe connected to the source of air. Usually, because there is a right-angle bend between the throat and the mouth, air cannot get out easily.

Students stand in the balanced position and let their heads drop backwards, mouths wide open. Now there is a clear passage for the air to come out. They take a deep breath and then expel the air as loudly as possible in an –*aaaaah* sound. Let them hold the sound for as long as they can. Tell them to visualize themselves as a trumpet spraying the sound on the ceiling.

3   Work on sounds, words and sentences

In this section there are activities for warming up basic English speech sounds, and for playing with words and sentences to develop sensitivity to stress, rhythm and intonation and increase students' confidence as they will English. You should emphasise the playfulness of these activities: they offer a chance to experiment with threatening and enjoyable context. And remind the or about how they feel about the activities the ones they enjoy have difficulties with, and the ones they have questions about.

a) Work on sounds

Vowels and consonants

Students take a deep breath and voice these vowel sounds on a long note: –*aaaaah* (aː) –*aaaaii* (aɪ) –*eeeee* (iː) –*iieeer* (ɪə) –*uuuuuu* (uː) –*uuueeer* (ʊə) –*eeeeeh* (e) –*eeeeer* (eə) –*oooooh* (uː) –*errrrrr* (ɜː) –*aaaauw* (aʊ). Then add initial consonant sounds to each of them: –*maaaaah*, –*naaaaah*, –*kaaaaah*, –*gaaaaah*, –*baaaaah*, –*paaaaah*, etc.

Pitch change

Take some of the above sounds and practise changing pitch on them: level, rising note, falling note, falling–rising note, rising–falling note. Students work in pairs and experiment with the different ways of saying these sounds.

Humming

Students hum on a –*mmmm*. They then add each of the vowels from the *Vowels and consonants* section above – for example, –*mmmaaaah*, –*mmmeeeee*, and so on. After this they repeat the procedure with a hum on –*nnnnnn*. They then work in pairs humming plus vowel but changing the pitch, as in the *Pitch change* section above.

Sound symphony

The above exercises are simply mechanical warm-ups. To add an element of invention, ask students, in groups of six, to devise a 'sound symphony'. They can use any of the sounds of English, plus any sound effects (whistles, lip popping, cries, barking, snoring, coughing, etc) to make up a one-minute sequence of sounds. The sequence may form a sort of story in sound, and should be interesting to listen to. Groups then perform their symphonies to each other. They try to interpret each other's stories or themes.

One of the groups did a marvellous performance, starting with a bell to signal the end of school, then sounds of running, street sounds, a door closing, music, glasses clinking, laughter … up to a final snore. And there was a lot of discussion (and criticism) of it by the other groups. (Charlene, teacher trainee)

b) Work on words

My name

Names are powerful words, like mantras. Repeating your own name in different ways somehow gives you possession of it. Speaking it to others in the class helps to affirm identity, and to relate to others' names too.

In this activity students explore their own names. They should try speaking their names in as many different ways as possible. Here are some possibilities:

- tasting it syllable by syllable: *Yo-shi-no Ta-ka-ha-shi*
- speaking it like a question
- speaking it as fast as possible
- making it sound as musical as possible

- whispering it, like a secret
- answering the question *What's your name?* in different ways:
  - as if answering when the teacher calls the roll
  - as if giving it when asked by a police officer
  - speaking it proudly and defiantly
  - speaking it as if it is a precious gift to someone special

When they have experimented for a few minutes, they go round speaking their names in different ways to others in the class.

This is a good activity to use towards the beginning of a course, when students do not yet know each other well. It is a good icebreaker, and sets up an atmosphere of easy familiarity. You should join in the activity too. Usually the natural follow-on from this is a discussion of the meanings or associations of different names.

I got a lot out of this activity. I think it's because we take our names so much for granted that we stop noticing them. But when I had to slowly 'taste' my own name, it was as if I'd never really heard it before. I got a similar reaction from the students when I tried it in class. (Monique, MA student/teacher)

You can follow up by giving each student the name of a famous English-speaking person: Jane Austen, Charles Dickens, Nelson Mandela, Hillary Clinton, etc. They experiment with different ways of speaking their new name, then go round introducing themselves to others in the class.

Speaking in numbers

Students work in pairs (A and B). Each is allowed to use the numbers from 1–10 only. Using the numbers as if they were real words, they have a conversation. For example:

A: One three five nine two?
B: Nine two. Nine two!
A: Six four eight!!
B: Four eight?
A: Four eight ten!

When they get used to mapping English-sounding sentence tunes onto the numbers, they change partners and continue. You can give more directions if you wish: for example, telling A that they are angry about something, and B that they are apologizing. Or by giving a context: A is a passenger on an aircraft and B is a flight attendant; or A and B are in a car arguing about which road to take ... Removing the need to think of real words means that students can focus on pronunciation features such as rhythm, stress and intonation. You can extend this kind of activity by using letters of the alphabet instead of numbers, or the vowels A E I O U, or limited vocabularies. For example, students might only be allowed to use the words *yes, , , you* and *good.*

When you suggested this activity, I thought it was crazy. p rc l er lik that? Why not us and have real conversations. I ea that the kids loved it it almost like a secret language d t co versations sounde g realistic -- a bit like surrealist t n

My favourite word

Ask students to choose their favourite English word, or one they particularly like the sound of. In pairs, they explore it in as many different ways as they can. They then change partners and repeat the activity. Here are some ideas:

- changing the intonation (rising, falling, rise–fall, fall–rise)
- changing the pitch (from high to low)
- changing the volume (shout to whisper)
- changing the mood (angry, disappointed, jubilant, bored, etc)
- cutting out all the consonants (eg *craving* – /eɪɪ/)
- cutting out all the vowels (eg *craving* – /krvŋ/)

This activity helps students to approach words from a new direction – by getting their mouth round the words in a physical not just a semantic way. It also encourages them to share their vocabulary so that they learn from each other.

We had plenty of laughs with this – words popped up I had no idea they knew: 'puddle', 'tacky', 'trophy', 'tiddler', 'grubby', 'atrocious' … And they really enjoyed just playing with them. I think they all gained in confidence – and probably learnt some new words too. (Bao, teacher trainee)

How many ways …?

Leading on from *My favourite word* above, ask students to work in pairs on the following list of words. Again, they are to find as many different ways of saying the words as possible.

Really	*Right*
Extraordinary	*Agreed*
Goodness	*Definitely*
Strange	*Quite*
Nice	*Unfortunate*
Incredible	*Pity*

They then try to construct short dialogues using some or all of these words with the pronunciations they think are appropriate. For example:

A: Really?
B: Definitely!
A: Extraordinary!
B: Quite.
A: Pity.
B: Agreed.

'Real' conversations are often cryptic and elliptical like this. These one-word expressions are also very useful to students because they can give the impression of fluent confidence in the language. What is more, students can have quite a lot of fun imagining, and sharing with the class, the unspoken topic of their 'conversations'.

This really caught on with one of my classes. I even heard their 'really's and their 'extraordinary's out in the corridor after the lesson. (Amin, MA student/teacher)

Mini-dialogues

Prepare some minimal dialogues such as these:

A: Who?	A: Time?	A: Tea?	A: Nice?
B: You.	B: Sorry.	B: Thanks.	B: Very.
A: Me?	A: Problem?	A: Here.	A: Exciting?
B: Yes!	B: Not really.	B: It's cold.	B: Wow!

In pairs, students try reading them in as many different ways as they can. To do this, it will help if they try to put the dialogues into a context: Who are these people? Where are they? What are they talking about? When they have tried out several interpretations, each pair performs its preferred version to another pair, who try to guess what the context is. You can develop the activity by asking students to extend each line of the dialogue by adding a few more words to make the context explicit.

One of the most inventive ones I got was the one about tea. The context is James Bond, held prisoner by Mr Big. After 'It's cold,' they went on:

Mr Big: Where do you think you are? A five-star hotel?
James Bond: Well. Why not? I'll have a large Martini instead – shaken not stirred!

Word beginnings and endings

Prepare some lists of words with the same initial consonant clusters. You need about 20 words for each sound. For example:

/skr/ – *scream, scrape, scrap, scratch …*
/tr/ – *trouble, trap, troops, trick, try, treat, trumpet, tremble …*

Students work in groups of six, preferably standing in circles, but the activity can also be done seated. Students will play with the words on their list. Here are some ideas:

- Going round the circle, each student speaks the next word on the sheet in any way they like. They read round the group, one word each, in order but as quickly as they can, without any faltering.
- Student 1 reads the first word loudly, student 2 whispers hers, student 3 reads it loudly, and so on. (Other ways of alternating include high/low pitch; silent mouthing/speaking aloud; mumbling/articulating extra clearly; etc.)
- One student starts with the first word then looks or points at any student in the group to read the next word.
- Students 'give' their word to another person in the group.
- As they speak the word, they add a gesture or movement.
- As they speak the word, they taste a flavour – sweet, sour, bitter, salty, etc, and give the word that flavour through the way they speak it.
- You set the mood by telling them how to read: disappointed, happy, angry, depressed, etc. They then read the words round the circle trying to convey this mood.

- You tell them the context in which they will be speaking the word. For example:
  You have just won the national lottery.
  You have just failed your final exams.
  Someone has just given you some bad news.
  You have just met an old friend for the first time in ten years.
  They convey their feelings in the way they speak the word.
- Students read three words at a time, as if they were a sentence. For example:
  Student 1:   Trouble trap troops?
  Student 2:   Trick, try, treat!
  Gradually a kind of surreal dialogue will develop. They can then extend to four or five words at a time.

You can do the same set of exercises with final consonant clusters. In this case, it is better to work with words containing the same vowel sound as well as the same final consonant cluster. For example:

/ps/ – *lips, chips, hips, zips, dips, sips, whips, tips …*
/ts/ – *pets, nets, sets, let's, gets, bets, jets, wets …*

This is a very rich activity. Students become really familiar with the words through frequent repetition, yet the repetition is not boring. Their pronunciation improves, especially rhythm and intonation, and they become confident of being able to speak words in a variety of ways. In many parts of the world, students have a tendency to suppress or omit final consonants. Because the final clusters carry important information in English (eg –*s*, –*ing*, –*ed*, etc), this omission seriously impairs comprehensibility. So it is worth doing this activity as a regular part of lessons. Because it can be done in so many different ways, it need not become boring.

Mini-poems

Either individually or in small groups, students prepare to perform minimal poems like the following:

> *The farmer's wife has no sewing machine*
> *So she mends clothes by hand*
> *Rip*
> *Strip*
> *Split*
> *Clip*
> *Snip.*
>
> *Father doing odd jobs about the house*
> *Thrash mumble*
> *Crash grumble*
> *Bash fumble*
> *Smash jumble*
>   *Stumble*
>   *Tumble.*

Farmer's impression of a tea party
Snicker
Snigger
Giggle
Gaggle
Chitter
Chatter
Flitter
Flutter
Flatter.
Alan Duff

This worked best when I got students to do it in groups of four. They decided who would read which words, rehearsed it, and came up with a really polished performance – with a long sequence of repeated 'flatter's at the end, dying away into silence. (Eleni, teacher)

They enjoyed it so much that we wrote some of our own, just choosing a sequence of initial clusters – starting with 'gr-' (grin, grit, grime, etc). (Charles, teacher)

Word symphony

Remind them of the exercise *Sound symphony* on p 29. This time, in groups of six, they are to prepare a word symphony on a given theme. (You can either set a theme for each group, or allow them to choose their own theme.) They must decide which words and phrases they will use – usually not more than 20 – and then work out how to combine these words in a kind of verbal tapestry which will convey their theme and be interesting to listen to. They can add sound effects and gesture if they wish.

Here is an example of a group of words on the theme of water:

cool, flowing, gushing, thirsty, drink, refreshing, our life, flowing, rivers, streams, springs, bubbling, the sea, rain, splashing, our food, lakes … (etc)

Students decide who will speak each word (one or more students together), how loudly parts of the symphony will be spoken, how much repetition there will be, whether they will have a kind of background chorus going on, etc (see p 48 *Making the text speak* for more details on orchestrated readings). It may be a good idea to set up this task in one lesson, allowing time for decisions to be made. Then you could ask students to rehearse it out of class and to perform it in the next lesson, with groups performing for each other and commenting on each other's performances.

Sometimes I get really funny ones – but sometimes they are very moving too, like the one a group did on the theme of hunger, and another group on the theme of child abuse. It seems that the kind of 'stream of consciousness' format frees up their creativity in the language. (Junko, teacher)

c) **Work on sentences**

Work on complete utterances, even short ones, offers more scope for developing sensitivity to stress, rhythm and intonation. These supra-segmental features of English are notoriously difficult to teach and are perhaps better handled as part of a voicework programme, where the emphasis is on meaning and speaker intention, than as part of a formal pronunciation course.

Tongue twisters

These can be a lot of fun provided they are used sparingly. You may notice that students have difficulty with particular sounds or groups of sounds. A little regular practice with tongue-twisters which feature these sounds can be beneficial. But don't overdo it! Here are some examples for particular sounds:

> *Red lorry; yellow lorry.*
> *Wrap the reels round the rubber leads.* } *(for l/r distinction)*
>
> *The sun is stronger on the south side of the station. (for /s/)*
>
> *He leapt along on his left leg alone. (clear l)*
>
> *The tall ghoul in the hall was appallingly bald. (dark l)*
>
> *Three thrifty thieves thought thankfully of thirty-three thousand. (for /θ/)*
>
> *Smooth breathing is soothing. (for /ð/)*

These are good for particular speech organs:

> *Pass the pens and pencils please.*
> *Where are the waterproof watches we wanted to wind?* } *(for lips)*
> *We watched the beautiful blue waves washing over the wreck.*
>
> *Leave the lazy lad alone.*
> *Lie on the pillow and swallow your pills properly.* } *(for tongue)*
> *The leading soldier had been shot in the shoulder with a laser.*
>
> *I think he sang a song at the bankers' congress.* } *(for soft palate*
> *The longer you linger here, the stronger the things will get.* } *and back of*
> *How much coal can you carry from Katmandu to Calcutta?* } *tongue)*

And these are good for general fluent articulation:

> *My organs of articulation*
> *Were a definite vexation,*
> *Until I said this silly rhyme*
> *Three times through.*
>
> *Articulatory agility*
> *Is the desirable ability*
> *To manipulate with dexterity*
> *The tongue, the palate and the lips.*

Writing on a railway train
Is very hard to do
For it bumps you up and down
And shakes you through and through.

Clickety clack
Down the track
Heading for the station,
I'll put my pencil and paper away
Till I reach my destination.

Like a rocket shot to a ship ashore,
The lean red bolt of his body tore
Like a ripple of wind running swift on grass
Like a shadow on wheat when a cloud blows past.

John Masefield

Shifting the stress

Prepare a set of sentences like the ones below, in which it is possible to place the stress in different places to change the meaning. Students work in pairs, taking it in turns to put the stress on different syllables. As they do this they should explain what difference it makes to the meaning. For example:

I put your CAR away in the garage next door. (It was your car, not your bike.)
I put your car away in the garage NEXT DOOR. (Not in our garage.)

I loved a woman very like you once.
I've been finding strange things in the forest.
I think it would be better not to meet for a time.
There is no good reason to blame yourself.
I don't want anyone to kiss me at the moment.
Do you think it's a good idea?
Please don't forget to feed the cat.
Do you have a better suggestion to make?
I saw Sam coming out of the disco with Sadie last Saturday night.

A possible extension of the activity is to ask students, in pairs, to decide on *two* syllables which could be stressed. For example:
Please DON'T forget to feed the CAT.

Getting the sentence stress right is a key factor in conveying accurate meaning in English, and this offers students an opportunity to experiment with it.

My class of 15-year-olds had a ball with this one! Lots of slightly risqué interpretations – but lots of fun too. And they did seem to get the hang of sentence stress too!
(Peggy, MA student)

Words and movement

Prepare a list of sentences or lines from plays and give one set to each student. Students work in groups of four. Each student adds a gesture or movement to a line as they speak it. Here are some possible lines:

I just can't believe that.
But what made you do it?
I shall never forgive you.
To be, or not to be; that is the question.
This is just too much!
Who exactly is that woman in the cupboard?

Before deciding on their interpretation for each line, groups should experiment with different ways of saying the lines. They need to decide where the main stress will come. Usually this stress would be marked by some kind of movement. When they come to speaking the lines, let them try it this way:

- First speak the line, then add the gesture or movement.
- Next, do the gesture first, then speak the line.
- Finally, speak and move at the same time.

Adding movement to speech helps to reinforce the impact of the line and to integrate the language by involving more than one sensory channel.

I think one reason they enjoyed this so much was that it released energy they are usually expected to keep under control. All too often English is just in the head or the mouth. Here they could integrate it with movement too – and that seems to have helped.
(Mei Hua, MA student)

The lists game

In pairs or groups of three, students compete to produce sentences containing the longest lists of items. For example:

There were grapes, and oranges, and apples, and bananas, and cherries, and grapefruit, and melons, and … and pomegranates.

They must be sure to give the right intonation to the items in the list – all the items have a rising tone except the last, which ends on a fall. It is this falling note which signals that the list is finished. Other possible lists are nationalities, animals, vehicles, clothing, types of food on a menu, types of drinks, etc. Apart from its enjoyment value, this helps students revise or extend sets of related lexical items.

Sentence lengthening

You will need to prepare a handout like the example below. Students work in pairs. They take it in turns to read through the sentences from the shortest to the longest. Draw their attention to the need to take enough breath to carry them through the sentences as they lengthen. Also note the way the stress in each sentence changes as items are added.

They lived together.

They lived together for a long time.

They lived together for a long time before he found out.

They lived together for a long time before he found out that she had deceived him.

They lived together for a long time before he found out that she had deceived him by lying.

They lived together for a long time before he found out that she had deceived him by lying about her age.

They lived together for a long time before he found out that she had deceived him by lying about her age, her friends, her income and her past.

They lived together for a long time in what seemed like perfect happiness until one day he accidentally discovered that she had systematically deceived him over and over again by lying about (among other things) her age, her friendships, her income and even her criminal past.

They lived together for a long time in what seemed like perfect happiness until one day last December he accidentally discovered that she had systematically deceived him over and over again by lying about (among other things) her age, her friendships, her income, her family background and even her criminal past, so he packed his bags.

They lived together for a long time in what seemed like perfect happiness until one day last December he accidentally discovered that she had systematically deceived him over and over again by lying about (among other things) her age, her friendships, her income, her family background and even her criminal

---

It is worth spending some time on this activity as it underscores the need to match breathing to 'thought-length', and to the chunking/phrasing of the sentence as it gets longer. There are, of course, some well-known children's rhymes based on the lengthening principle: if you are working with young learners, 'This is the House that Jack Built' is an obvious example. See also 'The Responsibility' (p 49).

I sometimes use this activity as part of grammar awareness raising. After we've done the speaking in pairs, I get them to work on another 'stem' sentence, like 'He likes swimming.' They have to come up with a set of progressively longer sentences based on it. The pair with the longest (correct) sentence, or with the largest number of sentences, wins. I can then use these sentences as input for the same activity with another class. (Sarah, teacher)

All-purpose phrases

You will need to prepare a list of common phrases like those on p 39. It helps if they are all associated with a particular context or mood. Students work in groups of about ten (or as a whole class if you have plenty of space to move around in). Each student is given one of the phrases and must learn it by heart. They then mix and move, saying (not reading) their phrases to other students, who reply with theirs. Almost any combination of the phrases will make sense. What the students have to do is speak their particular phrase with maximum effect. If you have more than one group, let them perform their improvised dialogues to each other.

Example 1

Come on!
We're in a hurry.
It's time to go.
Why all the rush?
What's the problem?
There's plenty of time.
We'll be late.
You're making me nervous.
What time do we have to be there?
For goodness' sake!

Example 2

It's so quiet.
Where is everyone?
There's no one around.
It feels strange.
What's happening?
I'm scared.
Let's get out of here.
Come on!
It's creepy in here.
What was that noise?

The activity gives them plenty of opportunities to repeat common phrases in English without the repetition becoming tedious. They should also be encouraged to discuss the contexts in which the dialogues might have been taking place.

Chants

Depending on the proficiency level of the students, you can either just give them a theme (silence; sleep; water; childhood; etc) or give them a theme and a number of shortish lines as in the example below. Students work in groups of five, and practise speaking the lines in any order. They can either do this by sharing the lines among them (two each) or by speaking the lines in chorus at the same time. They should speak the lines in a measured, calm voice, so that the chant washes over the listeners leaving a feeling of peace and warmth.

Theme: Friendship

Warmth and understanding.
A shoulder to cry on.
Sharing good times – and bad.
Always there; ready to help.
Laughter together.

No need for words.
Perfect understanding.
Trust in each other.
Sharing secrets.
So reassuring.

Again, there is a lot of opportunity for repetition but the random permutations of the lines create continuously changing effects, a bit like a kaleidoscope in sound. I have found that students enjoy constructing their own chants too. Topics that work very well include money, football, music and the English weather. I usually ask for groups to suggest three phrases each – then we vote on the best ones for inclusion in the chant.

There's a rat in the fridge!

You will need to prepare a set of utterances like those below. The important thing is that many of these can form 'adjacency pairs': that is, they can go together in a credible conversational exchange. For example:
A: Have you ever had a mystical experience?

Could be responded to:
B: Do you know who I am?   or
B: It depends what you mean.   or
B: Who cares?   and so on.

Students are all given a different sentence to work with. They should learn it so that they can speak it rather than read it aloud. They then circulate, saying their sentence to each person they meet. If that person's sentence 'fits', they have a mini-dialogue already. They note down each other's sentences and then continue. At the end, in the feedback session, students report on the sentences they found which 'fitted'. The following are examples of sentences you might give:

There's a rat in the fridge.	*Well, what difference does it make?*
Do you know who I am?	*My tie is in the waste bin.*
I'm sorry. You can't go in there.	*Well, there must be a reason for that.*
That's just not possible.	*It depends what you mean.*
Have you ever had a mystical experience?	*Who cares?*
I refuse to believe it.	*We're closed. Sorry.*
Sorry, I can't help you.	*I've got a thorn in my finger.*
You didn't tell me you were married.	*What's it doing in there?*
Would you like me to take it out for you?	*You should be ashamed of yourself!*

This activity offers numerous opportunities for re-combining sentences in different ways. In the feedback session, students should give a possible context for their exchanges as well as performing them for the others. For example:

A: I've got a thorn in my finger.

B: We're closed. Sorry.

Context: someone needs medical attention but the chemist has just locked up for the night.

One of the benefits they got from this one was that they realized how useful some of the 'ready-made' phrases (like 'Who cares?') were. As a spin-off activity, we made our own list of 'Lego' phrases, and then constructed our own set of utterances for the activity. (Bernard, teacher)

4   Working with texts

a) Jokes and folks

This set of activities is based on retelling a spoken or written text. You will probably need to remind the students that retelling does not mean verbatim memorization of the original. What they need to do is to recall the main points and to tell these in their own words.

Retelling jokes

You will need a small selection of jokes printed on separate handouts. You can begin by telling the class a short joke and asking several students to retell it. For example:

A middle-aged lady was dining in a fancy restaurant when she noticed a fly in her soup. She called over the head waiter and asked angrily, 'What's this fly doing in my soup?' The waiter put on his spectacles, peered at her bowl of soup for a moment then replied, 'I cannot be absolutely sure, Madam, but it appears to be drowning.'

Students then work in pairs. All the As are given one of the joke handouts; all the Bs get a different joke handout. They prepare to retell their jokes to each other. When they do the retelling, they should not read the joke, but tell it from memory. You may want to give them some tips on telling jokes – keeping the listener in suspense by tone of voice, by adding details, and pausing just before the punchline to add effect, etc. In a later lesson, ask each student to bring one joke they have heard to tell a partner.

Retelling newspaper stories

You will need to prepare a number of short articles from the newspaper. These should be human interest stories or stories about unusual incidents. Here are two examples:

A man narrowly escaped death after he became buried in a lorry that was filled with sand. He was finally freed after 90 minutes by firefighters from the nearby town of Sketchley.	A man took refuge up a tree when he was chased by a wild boar in a wild animal park in Essex yesterday. He called for help on his mobile phone. By the time the police arrived the boar had got bored and gone away. But the man was still up the tree, suffering from shock.

Students again work in pairs with a different article each. They commit the story to memory and then retell it to their partner. They should try to make it as interesting and compelling as possible.

Retelling anecdotes

Students work in pairs and take it in turns to tell each other an anecdote about themselves. This may be a recent incident or something interesting or dramatic which happened to them in the past. They then retell the story to each other. The student who told the story listens and corrects. After this, they change partners and retell the stories they have just heard from their first partners.

Introductions

Students work in pairs, preferably with a partner they do not know very well. They are given ten minutes in which to find out as many interesting facts about their partner as possible. They need to take notes on what they learn. Students then have to prepare a two-minute talk about their partner, introducing her to the rest of the class.

All the above activities require careful listening. Students can also learn a lot from each other about how best to involve someone in what they are telling. They are usually very quick to pick up on effective ploys used by their classmates.

I used the 'Introductions' activity at the beginning of the course and it proved a real icebreaker. We learnt a lot about each other, and it helped to build a good cooperative atmosphere from the start. (Huang, teacher)

b) Correcting

You will need to prepare copies of the text you decide to use. The example below is a poem, but other text-types could also be used.

> *Henry King*
> *(who chewed bits of string, and was early cut off in dreadful agonies)*
>
> *The chief defect of Henry King,*
> *Was chewing little bits of string.*
> *At last he swallowed some which tied*
> *Itself in ugly knots inside.*
> *Physicians of the utmost fame*
> *Were called at once; but when they came*
> *They answered, as they took their fees,*
> *'There is no cure for this disease.*
> *Henry will very soon be dead.'*
> *His parents stood about his bed*
> *Lamenting his untimely death,*
> *When Henry, with his latest breath,*
> *Cried – 'Oh, my friends, be warned by me,*
> *That breakfast, dinner, lunch, and tea*
> *Are all the human frame requires …'*
> *With that, the wretched child expires.*
>
> Hilaire Belloc

Give the students a chance to read the poem through silently. Then tell them you will read the poem to them but that you might make some mistakes. Each time you do, they should stop you. The first student to say 'stop' then has to read the line correctly. This will involve them putting heavy 'corrective' stress on the offending item. You then go back to the beginning of the poem and start again, making different mistakes. For example:

T: The chief defect of Peter King …
S: Stop. The chief defect of HENRY King …
T: The chief defect of Henry King,
    Was chewing little bits of rope …
S: Stop! Was chewing little bits of STRING.

In later classes a student can make the deliberate mistakes.

c) How to say it

I learnt the idea of stage directions from Cynthia Beresford. The source of the play – slightly rewritten – is unknown.

You will need copies of a short play or sketch like the one on p 43. As you can see, there are empty brackets before some of the lines. Students work in groups of four. They have to decide how these lines will be spoken and insert an appropriate word or phrase as a stage direction to the actor.

A slightly less demanding way of doing this activity is to give the students a list of stage directions which they must match with the appropriate lines. When they have supplied the stage directions, students work in groups of three and rehearse a performance of it.

Jane: (*slightly nervously*) I'll go and see. Two's company; three's a crowd.

(*Loud knocking at the door.*)

Robert: ( ) Who the hell can that be at this time of night? It's nearly midnight.

Jane: ( ) I'll go and see.

(*More knocking.*)

Jane: ( ) All right! All right! I'm coming!

(*Sound of door opening.*)

Jane: ( ) There's no need to knock so ... Oh my God! Jack! Whatever are you doing here?

Jack: ( ) Oh my darling! I couldn't stand it any more. I had to see you. I just had to come.

Jane: ( ) For goodness' sake keep your voice down. Robert's in the lounge.

Jack: ( ) I know he is. That's why I've come ...

Robert: ( ) Jane, who is it? Who's there?

Jane: ( ) It's ... It's ... It's only Jack.

Robert: ( ) Well don't keep him out there in the cold. Tell him to come in.

Jane: ( ) Jack! Jack! We can't do this. We can't!

Jack: ( ) Oh yes we can. Don't you worry darling. Just leave it all to me. Everything's going to be OK.

(*Sound of drinks being poured. Door opening.*)

Robert: ( ) Hello there, Jack. You're just in time for a drink. What'll it be?

Jane: ( ) He's not staying!

Robert: ( ) Of course he's staying. He never refuses a free drink, do you Jack? Whisky?

(*Sound of drink being poured.*)

Robert: ( ) Here you are, Jack. What ...? What are you doing with that gun?

Jane: ( ) Jack, are you crazy?

Jack: ( ) Oh no, Jane. I'm perfectly sane.

Robert: ( ) Now come on, old boy ... Just put the gun down, and let's talk.

Jane: ( ) Jack! Please!

Jack: ( ) No, Jane. This is the only way. We love each other and there's only one person standing between us.

Jane: ( ) Jack, please don't do it! Don't do it!

Jack: ( ) I must. Sorry about this, Robert. But surely you can see ...

Robert: ( ) Jane, for God's sake do something!

(*Loud gunshot. Screams. Sound of body falling and breaking glass.*)

Jack: ( ) Now, Jane, at last we're free ...

Jane: ( ) Oh, you idiot! You utter bloody idiot! Now what are we going to do?

(*Sound of police car siren. Loud knocking on the door.*)

d) Stretching the text 1

In this section there are a number of ideas for 'getting inside the text' by playing with it in various ways – all focused on the voice. These exercises require intense concentration, and careful listening to others as well as to oneself, in order to coordinate the reading. Students have to focus especially on rhythm and on fitting the sound to the sense. By deconstructing texts in these ways, the readers come to apprehend them in a different way from a 'normal' reading, which may often be superficial. The text is 'made strange' in order that it can be understood better when it is read 'normally' later.

In order to make these ideas concrete, most of them will be based on the same text – 'On a Tired Housewife', below. Obviously, the ideas can be applied to many kinds of text, however, and you will need to choose texts which are appropriate to your students' level and interests.

On a Tired Housewife

Here lies a poor woman who was always tired.
She lived in a house where help wasn't hired:
Her last words on earth were, 'Dear friends, I am going
To where there's no cooking, or washing, or sewing,
For everything there is exact to my wishes,
For where they don't eat, there's no washing of dishes.
I'll be where loud anthems will always be ringing,
But having no voice, I'll be quit of the singing.
Don't mourn for me now; no, mourn for me never,
I'm going to do nothing for ever and ever.'

Anonymous

- Students work in groups of four or five. One student reads the text up to the first punctuation mark. The second student then takes over and reads to the next punctuation mark, and so on. They should try to keep a smooth pace throughout, so that the switchover of voices doesn't break the rhythm of the poem.
- In pairs, students read alternate words. Again, they have to do this while sustaining the normal rhythm of the lines. You can do the same activity with students sitting in a circle, each one reading a word in turn.
- In groups of four or five, they take alternate lines and read the text speaking only the vowel sounds. Then they read only the consonant sounds. Finally they read it in normal mode.
- In groups again, students read in turn. As they come to a punctuation mark, they change position, or make a movement.
- A development of the previous activity is to ask them to sit in a circle. The first student reads to the end of the first 'thought length' (these are usually marked by a full stop or a semi-colon). She then throws a small ball (or a piece of paper screwed up into a ball) to another student in the circle. This student reads to the end of the next thought length, then throws the ball to someone else, and so on.

The ideas in this section are based on the work of Cicely Berry in her book *The Actor and the Text* (Virgin Books 1993).

- In pairs, one student stands behind another. The student in front begins to read the text. The one behind (who does not have the text) tries to shadow the one in front by repeating the words a fraction of a second later.

The students found these ways of reading very difficult to begin with. But after I'd explained again how focusing on one thing, maybe something a bit strange, could help bring other things into focus, the idea seemed to click. When we came back to a 'normal' reading, they were much more confident. (Han, MA student)

e) Stretching the text 2

Again, you will need to select an appropriate text (see *Stretching the text 1* above) and have sufficient copies for all students. The procedures below can be followed step by step, or you can select the most appropriate activities.

- In pairs, students take turns to read the text. First they read, taking a breath at the end of each line. In the second reading, they breathe at the end of every second line. They continue in this way until they are reading the whole text on one breath! (If they really cannot manage the whole text on one breath, let them draw breath after *dishes*.)
- Working in pairs, students take turns to read the text to each other. Each student reads it in three different ways: firstly in a flat, expressionless way; then in a highly exaggerated, emotional way; finally in their 'normal' voice. Students monitor each other's readings, and when both have finished reading, they discuss the effects they felt.
- Again in pairs, they read the text in the following ways:
    – Read the first word of each line aloud, 'think' the rest of the line silently.
    – 'Think' the first part of the line silently, and speak the last word only.
    – Read each line 'normally'.
- In pairs, each student in turn mouths the text silently, then speaks it aloud.
- In pairs, each student intones the text, almost like a chant. After a few lines, they allow their voice to slip back into 'normal' speech.
- In pairs, one student reads the text one word or phrase at a time, then stops. The other student then probes with questions about what has been said. For example:
A: Here …
B: Where? Where is here?
A: Here lies …
B: Who lies here? Who are you talking about?
A: Here lies a poor woman …
B: Why is she poor? What does she do? Why is she lying there? (etc)

The ideas in this section are drawn from Patsy Rodenburg's book *The Actor Speaks* (Methuen 1998).

I can vouch for the effectiveness of these kinds of 'aiming off for wind' activities. It really does seem that doing something in an unusually constraining way makes it easier to do it 'normally' later.

f) **Breaking down and building up**

For this activity you really need a text with plenty of strong, muscular, evocative vocabulary. It works particularly well with some of the Shakespearean sonnets. However, given that many students will not be familiar with the language of Shakespeare's time, I have chosen a poem by Ted Hughes as an example. It is about the crow, who reigns over the kingdom of death.

King of Carrion

His palace is of skulls.

His crown is the last splinters
Of the vessel of life.

His throne is the scaffold of bones, the hanged thing's
Rack and final stretcher.

His robe is the black of the last blood.

His kingdom is empty –

The empty world, from which the last cry
Flapped hugely, hopelessly away
Into the blindness and dumbness and deafness of the gulf

Returning, shrunk, silent

To reign over silence.

You do not give the students the complete poem till the end. To begin with, give each student a slip of paper with one of the nouns or verbs on it. For example:

PALACE	SKULLS	CROWN	SPLINTERS	VESSEL	BONES	FLAPPED

They spend some time speaking their word, tasting its sound quality, trying different ways of saying it. They then think about meaning: *PALACE* – what associations does this have for me? When did I last visit a palace? Would I like to live in one? They then move round saying their word in different ways to all the others in the group, till most students have experienced all the words. Then do the same for the adjectives and adverbs. For example:

LAST	FINAL	HANGED	EMPTY	HOPELESSLY	HUGELY	SHRUNK	SILENT

Finally, do the same thing for the function words:

IS	OF	THE	HIS	FROM	WHICH

AWAY	INTO	AND	OVER	TO

You then need to prepare a 'text' composed only of content words (nouns, verbs, adjectives and adverbs) with enough copies for all the students in the class. You should also insert punctuation in the 'text'. This will help students to understand what rhythm and intonation they might give when they read it.

For example:

> PALACE SKULLS. LAST SPLINTERS CROWN LIFE VESSEL THRONE? SCAFFOLD BONES
> HANGED THING. RACK FINAL STRETCHER! ROBE BLACK, LAST BLOOD, KINGDOM EMPTY,
> EMPTY WORLD. LAST CRY FLAPPED! HUGELY, HOPELESSLY – BLINDNESS, DUMBNESS,
> DEAFNESS. AWAY, SHRUNK, SILENT REIGN. GULF RETURNING; SILENCE AWAY.

In pairs, students try ways of reading this 'text' as if it were a normal text, giving sense to it through the rhythm and movement of it. They then join another pair and try out their readings on each other. At this point you may wish to get students to speculate about the subject matter of the poem.

You now prepare a similar 'text' using only the function words:

> HIS IS OF HIS. IS THE OF THE OF? HIS IS THE OF. THE AND? HIS IS THE OF! THE HIS IS THE
> FROM. WHICH THE AWAY INTO THE AND? AND OF THE TO OVER!

Students again experiment in pairs with ways of reading it so that it makes a certain kind of 'surreal' sense. They then try out their readings on other pairs.

Now prepare slips of paper, each one bearing one line of the actual text. (There are just twelve lines in this poem, so you might need to prepare two sets for a larger group.) Students move round trying to find lines which might fit with their own. They then form groups and try to reassemble the poem from the fragments. When they are satisfied they have the original poem, they perform it together.

This is based on an activity in Kristin Linklater's *Freeing Shakespeare's Voice* (Theatre Communications

Finally, give out copies of the original poem. Students compare their versions with the original, discussing any points of variation. They then perform the original. In doing so they should be reminded of the physical feel and weight of the words as they have experienced them in the earlier activities with this poem.

I don't know of any better way to help students 'get inside' a poem and really understand it. Their final performance of the original was amazing. (Janice, MA student)

g) Star for a day

Select a clip from a feature film. The clip should be two or three minutes long and should involve anything between two and five characters. It is best to choose a particularly dramatic moment from the film – for example, the scene when Rhett Butler leaves Scarlett O'Hara towards the end of *Gone with the Wind*. You will need to transcribe the dialogue and add any necessary screen directions. All the students are then given the text. They watch the clip once, discuss any points needing clarification, then watch it again. You now form them into pairs or groups with the same number of members as there are parts in the film script. They have to prepare a version of the clip, acting it out in the way they have seen the original actors do. They have a few minutes to rehearse; then they perform for the others.

The activity requires them to pay close attention to the way the actors in the film speak, especially their voice inflections and stresses, their movements and gestures.

I learnt this activity from Jim Kahny at LIOJ, Odawara, Japan.

The students love this one. It has never failed to throw up interesting performances, often from normally reticent students, and lots of discussion about how people speak. Not just what they say, but how they say it. (Susan, teacher)

h) Making the text speak

You will need to make a selection of texts which are suitable for your students'
level and which lend themselves to being performed orally. They may be poems or
prose fragments. Raps, jazz chants, dialogue poems, rounds, poems with a lot of
repetition all work well. (See the *Other useful books* section of the bibliography for
some sources of texts.) They should not be drama texts.

The object of the activity is for students, working in groups, to prepare a
performance of the text in a way that is maximally interesting to listen to. Here are
some ways of making their performance interesting. You may like to remind them
of these before they start:

- varying the voices in terms of volume, speed (including pausing), rhythmic
  patterning, pitch levels, intensity and mood
- varying the number of voices speaking at any one time: some parts may be read
  solo, others by two or more students speaking simultaneously
- special effects, such as having a background theme word or phrase being
  repeated softly throughout, or having an echo effect, or having overlapping lines
  spoken simultaneously as in a round, or adding sound effects or gestures

The groups need to be given enough time to discuss how they will perform the text
and to rehearse it together. Allow up to half an hour for this. And allow time for
discussion and evaluation of their performances too. When they have done this
activity with a few texts, they will begin to incorporate techniques they have learnt
from earlier performances and from the discussions. This vocal exploration of texts
leads students to a different way of understanding them from what they are
accustomed to in 'comprehension' work. In order to perform the text successfully,
they have to apprehend it aesthetically, from the inside, in a way which is
qualitatively different from comprehending it cognitively, from the outside.
Students who work with texts in this way usually gain enormously in confidence
and in vocal expressivity.

Here are two possible texts:

40	*LOVE*
middle	*aged*
couple	*playing*
ten	*nis*
when	*the*
game	*ends*
and	*they*
go	*home*
the	*net*
will	*still*
be	*be*
tween	*them*

Roger McGough

The Responsibility

I am the man who gives the word,
If it should come, to use the Bomb.

I am the man who spreads the word
From him to them, if it should come.

I am the man who gets the word
From him who spreads the word from him.

I am the man who drops the Bomb
If ordered by the one who's heard
From him who merely spreads the word
The first one gives, if it should come.

I am the man who loads the Bomb
That he must drop should orders come
From him who gets the word passed on
By one who waits to hear from him.

I am the man who makes the Bomb
That he must load for him to drop
If told by one who gets the word
From one who passes it from him.

I am the man who fills the till,
Who pays the tax, who foots the bill
That guarantees the Bomb he makes
For him to load for him to drop
If orders come from one who gets
The word passed on to him by one
Who waits to hear it from the man
Who gives the word to use the Bomb.
I am the man behind it all;
I am the one responsible.

Peter Appleton

This technique is described in detail in 'Choral Speaking' (Alan Maley), *English Teaching Professional,* Issue 12, July 1999.

One of the great assets of this activity is the discipline which the students are willing to impose on themselves in order to 'get it right' for performance.

… students will accept a degree of discipline and impose upon themselves a relentless standard of perfection which no one would ever dream of in the teaching context. In the overall context of theatre work, details of intonation, articulation, body movement are corrected to a degree which no other situation would allow.
(Dieter Schwanitz, teacher of German as a foreign language)

Concluding remarks

I hope that you will try out at least some of the activities in this section. Remember that activities involving voicework do not have to replace your other classroom activities. Rather they offer an additional, enriching dimension to working with the oral aspects of language. I hope you and your students will enjoy using them as much as I have.

Chapter 3 **Voice for personal growth**

Introduction

In this chapter, I would like to shift the focus away from the purely practical orientation I have concentrated on so far. Voice in teaching is of paramount importance. There can be no doubt about that. But voice carries over into more personal areas too. It can help maintain our physical and psychological well-being. It can relieve pain and sickness. It can take us on a voyage of discovery of our own spiritual nature. How far you will want to venture into these uses of the voice will depend on you. But it is important to understand that there is nothing threatening or insidious in any of this. Even if you decide to open yourself to areas of experience which could be called spiritual, there is nothing to be afraid of, and you are not required to subscribe to any particular dogma or set of beliefs.

All major world religions have used the human voice as a way into their spiritual centre. Whether we think of Tibetan overtone chanting, Gregorian chant, the call to prayer and the recitation of the Koran, Vedic chanting in the Hindu tradition, Gospel singing, the Russian Orthodox liturgy, or the role of the Jewish cantor – all have a similar function.

The role of the voice and sound in healing is likewise well attested. The curative singing of David to Saul may be purely apocryphal, but we all intuitively understand and relate to the properties of 'soothing' music. This is what mothers do instinctively when they sing lullabies to their children to help them sleep. And music, particularly Baroque music, has been shown to have a calming effect on disturbed or over-stressed patients, and even on animals. A comparable use of music is applied in Suggestopoedia as a way of lowering the threshold of resistance to the new language. In many pre-literate societies chanting and the use of percussive music is routinely used by shamans to bring about healing. In like manner, the wailing, keening and ululating which accompanies mourning in many societies seems to function as a way of purging grief. And blues singing has a similar therapeutic function, allowing us to tap the pool of melancholy and suffering we all share, and in doing so, to make it bearable.

But you may be asking yourself why the voice is such a powerful instrument for physical well-being, and for access to deeper layers of our consciousness. How exactly does it achieve its effects? It seems to work in three main ways:

1 The voice is sound, and sound is made up of vibrations and resonance. When we send out sound waves, they cause other things to vibrate too. Our bodies, for example, vibrate when we speak, and resonate in sympathy with the wavelengths we emit.

> *There is no greater and more living resonator of sound than the human body. Sound has an effect on each atom of the body, for each atom resounds.*
> Hazrat Inayat Khan

The human being is therefore likened to a very complex, unique and finely-tuned instrument. Every atom, molecule, cell, tissue and organ of the body continually broadcasts the frequencies of physical, emotional, mental and spiritual life. The human voice is an indicator of its body's health on all these levels of experience. It establishes a relationship between the individual and the wondrous network of vibrations that is the cosmos.

Olivea Dewhurst-Maddock

Therefore, by using our voices in particular ways, we can vibrate our bodies to bring them into harmony with the vibrations which surround them.

To sound the voice is to massage, oxygenate and vibrate ourselves internally from the inside out.

Don G. Campbell

2   The voice can also tap into our limbic system – the part of our brain which controls our emotional responses. As far as we know, language is not formed in this part of the brain. It originates in the neocortex, the new brain, which generates conscious thought. However, the limbic system or mid-brain does give rise to all the more instinctive sounds we make – cries of pain or joy, the humming and cooing sounds mothers make to their babies, and so on. These sounds of grief or ecstasy lie beneath cognitive language.

By using toning and chanting we can tap into this part of our brain with beneficial effects.

Our natural urges to belong ... stem from the old mammalian brain, the mid-brain. When we chant or hum for long periods, we can stimulate this limbic area to reduce stress and give us a sense of well-being. Toning creates a deep sense of being bonded within ourselves. We can reach a state of contentment in a safe and fully aware state of mind.

Don G. Campbell

3   Some uses of the voice can affect the brainwaves we experience. It is now well established that the human brain operates with different brainwaves at different times. These are:

- Beta waves (13–30 Hz – cycles per second). In a Beta state of rapid brainwaves we are fully conscious, awake, rational, and we perform our 'normal' mental activity.
- Alpha waves (8–13 Hz). These are slower waves which occur in states of relaxation, when we are awake but pleasantly content.
- Theta waves (4–7 Hz). These are very slow waves which take over when we are deeply relaxed, in a state of day-dreaming, meditation or in that halfway state of floating reverie which occurs just before we go to sleep. This is the state in which many people report having highly creative ideas, perhaps because the normal rational controls are suspended.
- Delta waves (0.5–4 Hz). The slowest waves of all, which occur when we are in deep sleep.

Because the brain adjusts to the wavelength of the sounds it receives (the technical term is 'entrainment'), it is possible to change the prevailing brainwave type by listening to certain kinds of music or using the voice. By inducing Theta waves, we can increase the degree of relaxation and open up to ideas and thoughts we would not have in our normal Beta wave state. It is interesting to note that the frequency of the electrical field between the earth and the ionosphere is also around 7.8 Hz. When we are in a Theta state, we have in a sense 'tuned in' to the basic earth frequency. You might like to notice your own feelings and mental state when you try out some of the activities suggested later in this chapter.

You can find further, more detailed information about these uses of the voice and their effects in the many books on the subject. I would particularly recommend Olivea Dewhurst-Maddock's *Healing with Sound*, Don Campbell's *The Roar of Silence* and Kay Gardner's *Sounding the Inner Landscape* (see annotated bibliography).

All this may well be true, but you will not find it relevant unless it works for you too. There is only one way to find out – and that is to try it. Do not expect miraculous results, but do not give up immediately either. You need to practise regularly over a period of time. If you regularly try at least some of the ideas outlined below, you will probably start to notice an improvement in body tone and mental alertness. So if you want to be 'keen of mind, light of step and bright of eye' why not give it a try? Remember that:

> *Your voice reflects your whole health – physical, mental and spiritual. The hallmarks of a healthy voice are versatility, sensitivity, warmth and purity of tone: clear bright and open with no hint of forcing or straining. Above all the healthy voice possesses vitality – the abundance of vital energy that can triumph over hardship, disappointment and pain.*
> Olivea Dewhurst-Maddock

I am certainly not suggesting that you try all the activities described in this last chapter. And you should not even contemplate trying them all at once! The reason for including so many activities is to allow you a degree of choice – to increase the likelihood of your finding something which works for you. If you are at all interested, and not everyone will be, I suggest you choose one or two which you feel comfortable with. Try them out for a few weeks before you decide whether or not to keep going with them. It is important not simply to try them once or twice and then switch to something else. They all take time to have an effect. It will be useful if you can get into the habit of monitoring your feelings and reactions after you have tried one of them. If, after trying them, you feel it has not been worth the effort, be reassured that there is nothing wrong with you! 'Different strokes for different folks' is the maxim to follow. What works for Jack may not work for Jill. And what works for you this year may change next year. Take it easy!

If things do work out, however, you should notice some very real benefits in terms of stress reduction, clarity of thought, better concentration, increased energy levels, and a general sense of well-being and feeling 'in tune' with life.

1 Activities without voice

Making sounds is the last stage in a long process which begins with a mental impulse, which is translated into muscular movements, the intake and expulsion of air, and the articulation of vibrations. The sounds are the tip of a very large iceberg. These largely silent activities help to get below the surface of the sound product – down into the processes which produce the sounds.

a) Just sitting

Most meditational systems require you to sit erect, while concentrating on something to the exclusion of everything else. So it is worth learning how to 'just sit'.

To be comfortably erect, you need a base to build your spine on. To do this, your pelvis needs to be above the level of your knees. Find a cushion which will support your pelvis. Sitting cross-legged in this posture, let your body find its natural point of balance.

A balanced posture requires very little effort to sustain and allows the major muscles of the body to relax. This relatively small expenditure of energy, coupled with the phenomenon of relaxation, produces a distinct feeling tone of softness, ease, and vibratory flow. It also generates a natural condition of alert awareness.
Will Johnson

Allow yourself to 'surrender the body to gravity, and yet remain as tall as you possibly can be.' (Will Johnson 1996)

When you are comfortably erect, close your eyes, and simply observe your breathing. Do not try to change your breathing to fit some idea you may have about what 'breathing properly' should be like. Just observe it as it is.

After five or ten minutes, begin to sway your torso gently from side to side. Gradually sway more and more until you almost lose your balance. Then slowly reduce your swaying until you naturally come to rest in the erect position again. Then rock gently forwards and backwards from the pelvis, gradually increasing the amplitude of your rocking. Reduce gradually until you come back to the erect position again.

Why do it? 'Life becomes easier when we make the enormous force of gravity our ally rather than our adversary.' (Will Johnson 1996 p 90.) Finding our physical point of balance helps find our mental balance too. Both are supports for the voice.

Try to monitor your feelings when you have tried this exercise. How do you feel physically, and in your mind? How well did it work for you? Did you have any problems with it?

b) Pranayama

Sit in an erect position, either on a chair or cross-legged. Press your right thumb against your right nostril, closing it off. Bring your second finger to rest lightly on the left nostril. Breathe into your left nostril. When you have taken a full breath, release your thumb, and close your left nostril with your second finger. At the same time, release the air down your right nostril.

Then reverse the process, breathing in through your right nostril and out through your left, blocking the other nostril as you do so. Try doing this with alternate nostrils till you get the hang of it.

Then, as you breathe in, count to five, and release your breath to the count of ten. Do this ten times each side. Try to visualize the air as a stream of energy moving through you from one side to the other. If you find it helps, keep your eyes closed as you do it. Then rest. As you become used to doing the exercise, gradually increase the length of in-breath and out-breath, but always keep the ratio 1:2 (eg six in, twelve out; seven in, fourteen out; etc). But remember not to overdo it: this is not the breathing Olympics! You need to use your finger or thumb on the out-nostril to control the outflow of air, and if you need to slow the intake of air too.

Why do it? The concentration calms you down and clears your mind. You should feel energized after it. And your breath control will improve dramatically – with knock-on effects for your voice.

When I first tried this, I had a bit of difficulty matching the length of the breath to the count. Gradually, by experimenting with degrees of pressure on the nostril in use, I found I could control the flow of air better. I also became more aware of the cool feel of the incoming air as it hit the highest point in its curve.

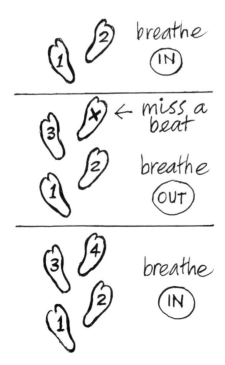

c) Walking meditation

You can do this whenever you have to walk somewhere: to the bus stop, to the shops, around the campus, taking the dog for a walk. Try to make it a habit. Walk at a brisk but not racing pace. Lead off with your left foot, starting your in-breath through the nose as you do so. Your in-breath will last four paces: left, right, left, right (one, two, three, four). Breathe out through the mouth on the next three steps: left, right, left (one, two, three). The next right is 'empty'; that is you don't breathe. Then you start a new sequence with your next left foot. Feel the rhythm take you over. Swing your lower arms in turn to match the foot movements (left leg – right arm). Keep it all nice and loose and fluid. Concentrate on just doing it; discard other distracting thoughts.

Why do it? It improves your concentration and physical coordination, especially breath control, which has beneficial effects on your voice. And you will find you can walk long distances without getting tired. It is also very simple, and can be incorporated into one of your everyday activities: no apparatus, no special room – just walking. My students in Singapore were amazed at quite how different 'just walking' felt when they did it this way.

d) Tao exercises

Here are eight Tao exercises which are easy to do and only take 20–30 minutes a day.

Gathering energy

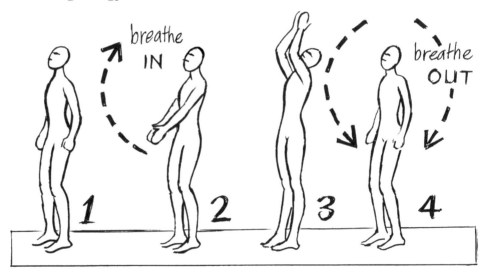

Stand in the balanced position: relaxed yet erect, shoulders down, knees lightly flexed, feet shoulder-width apart. Arms by your side. Face relaxed. Smiling gently. Place the top of your right hand lightly on the palm of your left hand and move your arms up to a point mid-way between your navel and your pubis. (This is where your energy centre, your 'chi' is located.) On an in-breath, slowly continue raising your hands till they are above your head, straightening your knees as you do so. Then, on the out-breath, slowly sweep them down to your sides and back to the starting point, flexing your knees again. Visualize yourself gathering energy in your hands and bringing it to your 'chi'. Do this five times.

Stretching your wings

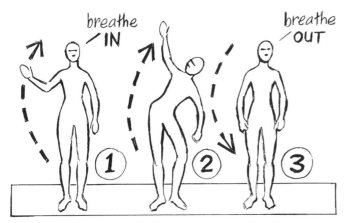

Start from the balanced position. Slowly raise your right arm on the in-breath, bending your trunk to the left as you do so and straightening your right leg. Keep your eye on the fingertips. Stretch over as far to the left as you can with comfort. Then come back to centre on the out-breath as you flex your knees again. Repeat the process with the left arm. Do the complete movement five times on each arm.

Side to side

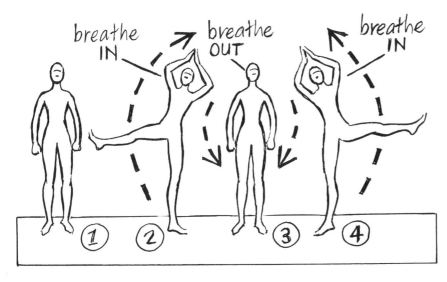

Start from the balanced position. On the in-breath, raise both hands slowly till your fingertips touch above your head. At the same time, raise your right leg horizontally to the side and bend your trunk to the left. On the out-breath, return slowly to the starting position. Then repeat the movement, raising your left leg. Do this five times on each leg.

Pelvis rolling

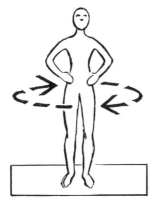

Stand in the balanced position, with hands resting lightly on the top of each hip, thumbs to the rear, fingers to the front. Rotate your pelvis slowly towards the front from right to left as you take a breath. On the out-breath, roll your pelvis backwards towards the right. Do this five times. Then reverse the process – rolling first to the front right, then returning to the back left. Visualize your pelvis as resting on a big ball-bearing. Make sure only your pelvis moves (not your shoulders, head and knees).

Circling the sky

From the balanced position, drop forward from the waist, letting your head and arms hang loose. Your hands should be the same distance apart as your feet. Imagine you are holding a bamboo pole in your hands. This means your hands will always be the same distance apart. Slowly, on the in-breath, raise your arms to the right while rotating your trunk from the hips. When you reach the top, you will be leaning back – and your lungs will be full. As you go down to the left, release the air. Then reverse the process, raising your arms to the left and lowering to the right. Repeat the movement five times on each side.

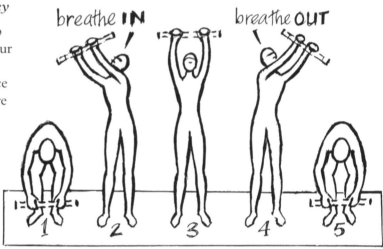

The robot

Start from the balanced position. On the in-breath, slowly raise your right leg till the thigh forms a right angle with the lower leg. Let the lower leg hang loosely. At the same time, raise your right arm till the lower arm forms a right angle with the upper arm. On the out-breath, slowly return to the starting position. Your hand should reach 'bottom' at the same time as your foot touches the ground. At this point, your lungs should be empty.

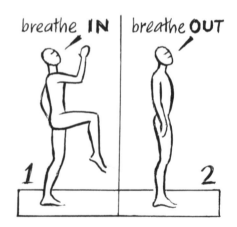

Flying away

Stand in the balanced position. Raise your arms to the side to shoulder height, hands loose. On the in-breath, slowly raise your right foot towards the front. As you release your breath, move your leg back till it forms a straight line with your back and head, bend your knee and stretch your head and body forward. Keep them in alignment, and look at the floor (not the wall) in front of you. Slowly come back to the starting position on a new in-breath. Repeat the sequence alternately five times on each leg.

Moving meditation

Starting from the balanced position, raise your hands, palms facing the front, till they are on a level with your eyes. At the same time, breathe in and flex your knees. Then, on the out-breath, move your hands down, palms now facing the ground, as if you were gently pushing the air down. At the same time, straighten your knees. When your hands are by your sides, and your lungs empty, repeat the process. Keep your eyes gently fixed on a spot dead ahead throughout. Do it twenty times. Feel the slow, gentle rhythm take you over.

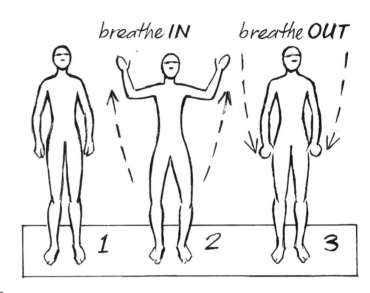

Why do them? They are wonderfully relaxing and leave you feeling calm and physically and mentally restored. They develop a very high degree of control over your breathing and help to coordinate your breathing and movement. All excellent for voicework.

These are the exercises I do myself, partly because they are not too energetic or physically taxing for a person of my age! Also, I find I can do them almost anywhere, which is important as I travel quite a lot and often stay in hotels. And they are so simple, once you've got the hang of them. I'd tried a number of other routines before, including yoga, but this sequence seems to suit me. I find they are a great way to start the day. See if your experience matches mine.

I found these exercises in Stephen Cheng's *The Tao of Voice* (Destiny Books 1991) and found further inspiration from his workshop at the Mind, Body, Spirit event in London in 1998.

e) Thinking the sound

Start from the balanced position, eyes closed, with your hands hanging loosely by your side. Think of your hands and arms as great wings. Then visualize them moving slowly upwards in a sweeping movement like an eagle flapping its wings. When they are straight above your head, visualize sweeping them slowly down again. Remember, you do **not** move: you simply imagine yourself going through these movements.

Then, still with eyes closed, imagine that your voice is moving through a sequence of these sounds: –*hmm*, –*oh*, –*ah*, –*eh*, –*ee*. Do not make any sound: just 'think' the sounds until they are flowing smoothly through your mind.

Then, still with eyes closed, put the two visualizations together. With hands by your sides think the sound –*hmm*, then raise your arms to a 45-degree angle as you move to –*oh*. Then to 90 degrees as you move to –*ah*. Then to 45 degrees above your head on –*eh* and directly above your head as you reach –*ee*. Remember, you do not actually move or make any sounds – it is all in your mind.

Why do it? This visualization exercise is akin to those that athletes, actors or singers often use when they 'rehearse' their actions. The activity develops an acute awareness of your body and usually leads to enhanced performance when you do move and make the sounds. (See also Chapter 2 p 22 *The inner workbench*.)

This is slightly adapted from an activity in Don Campbell's *The Roar of Silence* (Theosophical Publishing House 1990).

When I first used this with my theatre studies students they reported that they could sense their arm and shoulder muscles 'wanting' to move as they visualized moving them. This muscular state of readiness is similar to what you can feel happening to your tongue, throat and mouth if you get ready to say a word, then stop yourself from speaking it. You might like to try a simple experiment before you do this activity. Look at your right hand. Then have the intention to move your third finger – but don't actually move it. What do you notice?

f) Nature listening

Find yourself a quiet spot, somewhere away from people and unnatural noise. The top of a hill or mountain, the banks of a lake or river, or the sea shore are good places, but anywhere will do – even a deserted supermarket car park. The best time of day for this is early morning or early evening before it gets dark.

Stand quietly with your eyes closed, and simply become aware of your surroundings through your ears and the sensation of the air on your skin.

Take your time over this. Then open your eyes and really look at what is around you. Feel yourself tuning in to your surroundings.

When you feel ready, just open your mouth and let the sound pour out of you. It doesn't matter if you don't sound like an opera singer – just sing: sing yourself. Sing your surroundings. Sing yourself into your surroundings. You will be surprised at the power and freedom of your voice when you let it go.

Then sit quietly for a while, letting the atmosphere take over.

Why do it? All too often in our daily lives we are holding ourselves in. We rarely give our voices the chance to open up fully. But when you are alone, tuned to your surroundings, you can allow your voice to sing the person you really are.

My favourite spot for this is a rock which juts out into a small river in the south-west of France. It is a magical place at dusk or dawn, and it makes me feel as if I am merging with it – when I allow it to. But you don't have to go to France to find a place that suits you. There are very few places which don't have quiet spaces nearby.

2 Toning/chanting activities

a) Toning your body

Sit in a comfortable, erect position. Cross-legged on the floor is fine, but so is sitting on a firm chair, soles of the feet flat on the floor. Take a nice deep breath, but don't force it. Then start to hum on a low note – as low as you can manage comfortably. Just let it come out. Never mind if it is not particularly melodious! Go on doing this for a few minutes, then move the sound to a higher pitch and slide back down again. Then rest the palms of your hands gently on your cheekbones – feel the vibrations. Try feeling the vibrations on your scalp, your forehead and your chest too. Just be aware of how the sound is vibrating your body.

b) Nahn

Sitting comfortably erect, close your eyes, take a deep breath and begin to make the sound *nahn* over and over on as long and low a note as you can manage with comfort. (Each time you tone the word, it should last for the whole of one breath.) Keep this going for about 10–15 minutes. Just let the sound take you over. As you go on making the sound, reflect on the muscles you are using to make it; feel the parts of your body which are vibrating, see the pictures the sound throws up in your mind. Then surrender to the sound again, gently pushing away any thoughts that come to distract you.

You may feel like a bit of a 'nahner' doing this! When I do the reflective part of the activity, I find the fact that the word has no content, no meaning, is in fact helpful because my mind starts to fill it with meanings and associations. Sometimes this makes it quite a problem to get back into the phase where I have to give in to the sound alone, while all the colours, shapes and thoughts are jostling for my attention. See how you find it yourself.

c) Why?

Sit comfortably erect. Then on one breath make the following sequence of vowel sounds. Make the sounds on a low note and glide slowly from one to the next (but make sure each sound is made separately before you glide to the next):

–oo (as in *mood*)
–oh (as in *cope*)
–aw (as in *awesome*)
–a (as in *action*)
–eh (as in *head*)
–ih (as in *in*)
–ee (as in *feel*)

Do this a few times until you feel the overall 'shape' of the sequence. Notice which parts of your body vibrate with each of the sounds. Spend a bit of time on this. It may help to do the sequence in reverse order – this sometimes makes it easier to notice where the sounds are coming from. When you have experimented for a time, go back to simply repeating the whole sequence on each breath you take. As you begin to experience the sequence as one long glide of slowly changing sound, you may notice that it forms the word *why*.

One of my students reported that this felt like a sort of 'sound-gestalt' experience. At one instant she would 'feel' the word *why* as she did it. At the next, she found she was perceiving each sound as separate from the next. And her perceptions flipped back and forth as in a gestalt drawing which is seen now this way, now that. See whether your experience matches hers.

d) Healing sounds

Taoist teaching believes that there are certain sounds which, if they are chanted, improve the function of particular bodily organs or relieve pain or stress in them.

Lungs

Sit with your hands on your thighs. Concentrate on your lungs. Slowly raise your hands towards the front, palms upwards towards the ceiling, until your hands are above your head. As you look at your hands, inhale, then exhale on the sound *–sssss*. When your lungs are empty, lower your hands and breathe normally. Repeat the sequence five or six times.

Kidneys

Sit with your hands resting on your thighs, palms down. Then bring your legs together, clasp your knees and lean forward. Lift your head slightly, take a deep breath and exhale on the sound *–wooooo*. As you do so, pull in your abdomen towards your kidneys. Repeat the sequence several times.

Liver

Stand in the balanced position. Raise your arms slowly out from your sides and over your head, keeping your eyes fixed on your hands. Link your fingers and turn the palms to face the ceiling. Take a deep breath. As you exhale, push upward with your right hand only (keep the fingers of both hands linked) and make the sound *–shhhhh*. Repeat this several times.

Heart

Do the same as for the liver, only this time push up with your right hand and make the sound *–haaaaw*.

Spleen, stomach, pancreas

Stand in the balanced position. Press your fingertips into the area between your ribs and your navel, slightly to the left of centre. Take a deep breath. As you exhale, make the sound *–whoooo*, while pushing in your stomach muscles and looking slightly upward.

The full works

Lie down on your back with your eyes closed and your arms by your side with the palms upwards. Take a full breath and release it to the sound *–heeeee*. You let the sound go by baring your teeth and letting the sound escape from the corners of your mouth. As you do so, you slowly flatten first your chest, then your solar plexus, then your abdomen. Visualize your body being rolled flat by a giant rolling pin.

e) Having a good groan

You need to find a space where you will not be disturbed (see *Nature listening* on p 59). Stand in the balanced position. Close your eyes. Start to tune in to your body – feel your heartbeat, the weight of your hands, the rhythm of your breathing. Feel your feet in contact with the earth. Relax your jaws and let your body groan through your mouth. Feel the sound rising up through you from your feet. Groan as loudly and as long as your body wants to. Just let go and allow the sound to come out.

I once went to a shamanic healer who, as part of the treatment, gave me an extremely vigorous and deep body massage. She told me that any time I felt a groan coming, I should let it go – that was part of the treatment. The groans were the vocal expression of the tensions and deep-seated pains in my muscles and joints. I was a bit sceptical to begin with but, as the session went on, I found myself letting go vocally more and more. At the end, I felt as if I had literally groaned my pain and tension away.

f) Coming home

Stand in the balanced position, eyes closed. As you breathe in, feel yourself drawing energy from the earth through your feet. On the out-breath, release this energy through your heart; feel it suffusing your whole body. On the next breath draw the energy down from your head, again releasing it through your heart. Continue to do this, alternating between feet and head, till you have established a gentle rhythm and can really visualize the flow of energy. Then begin to chant the word *home* in a low register, so that you can feel your chest and heart area vibrating as you release the energy. Keep this going for at least five minutes.

g) Releasing the pain

Lie down in semi-supine (see p 2), eyes closed. Just allow your body to relax. Adjust your position if necessary. Then scan your body in your mind's eye, one area at a time, noting any aches or pains. Concentrate on one particular area where you are experiencing pain. Try to visualize the pain as a colour, a shape, a texture, till you are really in touch with it. Then visualize your in-breath as a stream of light entering your body and filtering into every part of it. Direct the light to the area of pain. As you breathe out, let some of the pain drain away. After you have done this for a few minutes, add the sound *–aaaaah* to your out-breath. Feel the vibration loosening the pain and helping it to float away in a bubble of light.

You can do this same exercise to get rid of psychological pain. All of us have had the experience of being misunderstood or wrongly treated by someone, or of brooding on a particular problem, which saps our energy. When this happens to you next, try visualizing the problem and singing it away in a bubble of light, or feeling it drain out of you along with the sound.

h) Overtones

The best-known overtone chanting is practised by Tibetan monks. If you have never heard it, it is well worth listening to an audio cassette. (For example, *Tantric Harmonies*, The Gyume Tantric Choir, Spirit Music, Boulder, Colorado.) It is difficult to describe the effect in words but essentially what happens is that, while chanting on a very low note (the fundamental), a number of harmonics start to be heard higher in the voice range. The effect is that one person seems to be singing two notes simultaneously. Even if you don't manage to achieve this effect yourself, you can still benefit from the kind of chanting which produces it.

Here is what you do. You can do it either standing or sitting. Purse your lips slightly, as if you were about to sip from a straw. Yawn and hold your lower jaw down, but still keep only a small opening in your lips. Visualize your mouth as a huge cave in which sounds can roll around and echo. Then on each out-breath start to make this sequence of sounds, starting in a very low register: *–oo –oh –aw –ah –a –eh –ih –ee*. (See *Why* on p 61.) Practise doing this until the sequence is flowing smoothly. Be aware of how your tongue is moulding each sound and how the shape of your mouth-chamber is changing as you move through the sequence. There is no need to move your lips: allow your mouth to do the work. Then move your voice up into your nose. After a time you may (if you are lucky!) become aware of a higher silvery note above your lower fundamental.

i) Chants

The repetition of short chants has been practised by religious groups and by healers since time immemorial. Although you can do these on your own, some people find they get more out of chanting if they do it in a group. You may like to try chanting some existing chants, like the examples below. To get the best effect, they should be chanted over and over again. Later you might consider inventing your own chants to suit your mood or purpose.

Wind in the hills.
Wind in the trees.
Wind on the water.
Wind in my hair.
Wind, wind, wind:
Feel the earth breathing, breathing.

Morning light.
Morning light.
Morning new-minted.
Good morning, Morning.
How shall I spend you?

Living to learn.
Learning to live.
Learning to laugh.
Learning to love.
Learning to lose.
Learning to live.
Learning to live.
Living to learn.
A. M.

j) Mantras

A mantra is a word or a short phrase used as a prayer or invocation. For those who use them, mantras have a special power which is intrinsic to the words themselves.

In the original mantric languages, the name of a thing is the sound of the thing itself.
Jill Purce

It isn't necessary to know what the mantra means for it to have an effect, for it is the sound itself, without intellectual translation, that touches the spirit.
Kay Gardner

Part of the power of the mantra lies in its rhythmical repetition, in which 'the sounds and rhythms of the words evolve beyond their definition' (Don G. Campbell 1989). Yet, as they are chanted repeatedly, the words take on overtones of meaning which arise from their interaction with our thoughts and associations.

All words hold the same power to disappear into sound and then reappear with meaning.
Don G. Campbell

… it is repeated not for the sake of repetition, but for the sake of purification, as an aid to all effort. It has no empty repetition. For each repetition has a new meaning …
Mahatma Gandhi

One of the best-known mantras is *Om* or *Aum*, used both by Buddhists and Hindus. It is interesting that to say *Aum*, our voice starts in the back of the mouth and has to traverse the cave of the mouth, ending with the closing of the lips – a kind of symbolic journey in sound. Here are some other well-known mantras from different traditions:

Om mani padme hum.
Om. Shanti, shanti, shanti.
Om tare tutare ture swaha.
Kyrie eleison, Christe eleison, Kyrie eleison.
Eli, eli, elu.
Ya-salaam.

You may like to try one of these for yourself. All you need to do is find a quiet place where you will not be disturbed and begin chanting your chosen mantra. It helps if you close your eyes but it is not essential. Simply go on repeating the mantra. You may find it helpful to set yourself a time limit – perhaps five minutes to begin with, then progressively lengthening it if you find the activity useful to you.

An alternative way to use mantras is not to speak them aloud but to rehearse them in your mind's ear. If you found *The inner workbench* idea useful (see p 22), you may prefer to do it this way.

In this section I have drawn upon ideas from Don Campbell's *The Roar of Silence* (Theosophical Publishing House 1989), Olivea Dewhurst-Maddock's *Healing with Sound* (Gaia Books 1997) and Kay Gardner's *Sounding the Inner Landscape* (Element Books 1997).

Postscript

As I mentioned earlier, there is no point in trying to do all these exercises. Choose something which feels right for you – and persist with it at least for long enough to give it a chance to work. And remember to be kind to yourself; don't expect too much too soon. Trying too hard can defeat the object of the exercise. Remember that we are all different; some people will get a real buzz out of a technique, others a mild feeling of greater tranquillity, others nothing except a pain in the joints! If I have persuaded you that it is at least worth trying some of these activities, I shall be amply rewarded. Good luck!

Chapter 4   Care and maintenance of the voice

Introduction

Voice is our most precious asset, the resource without which we could not work at all. We should therefore be concerned to keep it in good condition. This chapter explains what the principal symptoms of voice disorder are and their causes. It will also suggest ways of taking care of our voices.

The most common problems teachers experience with their voices are:

- dry mouth and throat
- hoarseness and scratchy voice
- excessive throat clearing
- persistent throat or neck pain
- feeling of having a lump in the throat
- double voice (diplophonia – when the voice wobbles between two pitch levels)
- chronic laryngitis
- breathy voice
- gravelly voice
- unnaturally low pitch
- unnaturally high pitch
- diminution of pitch range and flexibility
- loss of volume even when trying to speak loudly
- voice fatigue
- loss of voice (aphonia)

Voice problems can usually be traced to one of three main causes: environmental, physical and self-induced.

1   Environmental problems

We live in a world where clean air is a rarity, where silence is virtually unknown and where our working conditions may oblige us to hold unnatural body postures over long periods. These are the kind of stressors which the environment imposes on the voice.

a)   Air quality

Dust
Dust particles cause irritation and inflammation of the mucus membranes, and may lead to infection, all of which can provoke vocal problems.

Remedies:
- Avoid dusty environments altogether.
- Keep windows closed if you are in a particularly dusty area.
- Ensure teaching rooms are regularly dusted, preferably with a damp cloth, and swept or swabbed down.
- Insist on dust-free chalk, if you use chalk at all.
- For journeys in urban environments, wear a face-mask.
- Breathe through the nose rather than through the mouth in dusty environments because the nose can trap dust particles.
- Drink plenty of fluids!

Fumes
- petrol fumes from motor vehicles and chemical fumes from industrial plants such as oil refineries
- fumes from marker board pens, cleaning fluids or sprays, insect sprays and disinfectants

Remedies:
- Be aware; be cautious.
- Keep the windows closed in polluted areas.
- Don't inhale any dangerous substances.
- Drink a lot (preferably water!).

Smoke
- wood smoke, coal smoke (especially the brown coal smoke produced in domestic heating in central Europe)
- tobacco smoke (the number one culprit!)

Remedies:
- Stay away from smoke.
- Drink lots of water.
- Institute a 'no smoking' policy in the staffroom.

Humidity
- In environments with unduly low or high humidity, our voices will be affected: if the air is too dry, the surfaces of the throat and mouth become dry and inflamed.
- If the air is too humid, it may cause excessive mucus to be formed, so that we are constantly clearing our throats or blowing our noses.
- Many teaching environments are affected by air-conditioning or central heating, both of which can lead to excessively high or low levels of humidity in the air.

Remedies:
- Buy a hygrometer, which will tell you what the relative humidity is.
- In dry rooms, you can install humidifiers, or more cheaply, simply keep bowls of water on the window sills, or pot plants which stand in saucers of water.
- In humid areas, air-conditioning usually lowers the humidity, but sometimes it lowers it too much.
- If your room is too dry because of central heating, put wet cloths or towels on the radiators, or use bowls of water.
- Drink plenty of water.

b) Noise

The problem
- classroom noise: scraping chairs, etc
- traffic noise (even through the night)
- construction work
- aeroplanes taking off and landing
- radios and TVs left on as 'background'
- the tinny syncopations coming from other people's personal stereos
- the muzak played in stores and shopping malls
- the more subtle, largely unnoticed sources of sound such as refrigerators, tube lights, air-conditioners, fans and computers, which all emit a hum

Remedies:
Not many, unfortunately. But being aware can help you not to increase noise levels, and to seek out quieter environments at least some of the time.

c) Human environment

The problem
- We may have to adjust to speaking to people who are either very close to us or rather far away.
- The 'cocktail party effect', which arises whenever a group of people are talking among themselves. In order to make themselves heard, speakers raise their voices slightly. This causes others to raise theirs, until everyone is speaking at the tops of their voices. This causes voice strain and sore throat.

Remedies:
- Avoid situations where a lot of people are talking at once, such as parties, crowded bars and discotheques.
- Never attempt to talk over other people (especially in class).
- Devise classroom strategies to obtain silence without shouting.

d) Room acoustics

The acoustic properties of the spaces we teach in may also impose unnecessary strains on our voices.

Some spaces are 'dead': the sound seems to be absorbed completely before it reaches the listeners. This makes teaching in them really hard work and can lead to voice strain. The dead acoustic may result from the shape of the room: long, narrow, low-ceilinged rooms are especially bad. Or it may depend on the materials the room is made of. Carpeted rooms with curtains and other soft furnishings can really soak up the sound, as can walls lined with books.

Remedies:
- Get rid of as much of the carpeting and soft furnishings as possible.
- If the room is very long and narrow, you might be able to use only part of it, so that your voice does not have to travel so far.
- Pronounce your consonants especially clearly, since this will enhance clarity.

At the other extreme are spaces with a very 'bright', clangy acoustic, in which the sounds are excessively sharp and may even echo. These spaces are usually large, high-ceilinged rooms with lots of hard exposed surfaces (wood, stone, concrete, tiled walls and floors, large areas of plate glass, and often with metal beams). They are very tiring to teach in.

Remedies:
- Cover as many of the surfaces as possible with more absorbent materials – carpets, drapes, screens, etc.
- Concentrate your teaching in a smaller area, preferably screened off from the rest of the room.
- Installing a false ceiling, though expensive, can also bring about a dramatic improvement.

2   Physical problems

a)   Ageing

As we grow older, our voices change.

- Boys' voices drop by an octave around the time of puberty.
- Girls' voices also deepen with age, though less dramatically.
- Men's voices continue to get deeper with age until about 70.
- Women's voices also tend to become deeper as they get older (in late old age the voices of the two sexes are often virtually indistinguishable).
- Older people tend to speak more slowly than younger people and their voices may lose much of their expressive power and volume.

Many of these changes are inevitable. However, as we have seen earlier, voice and posture are intimately linked. Older people often tend to 'let go': they lose their erect posture and become stiff and bent. Except in the case of actual physical disease, this is not at all inevitable. Actors in particular avoid the decline in the power of their voices by maintaining an erect posture. 'When the spine goes, everything goes,' as one actress remarked, or as the old adage has it, 'You are as old as your neck.' The work you have done in this book, if continued, will ensure that you retain your full vocal capacity well into old age.

b)   Infections/allergies

Allergic conditions
These seem to be on the increase, perhaps as a result of human abuse of the environment. Some allergies cause inflammation of the nose and throat, which leads to constriction and so to hoarseness or blocked nasal passages.

Remedies:
- If you suffer from an allergic reaction, seek medical advice.
- Avoid patent medicines – many of them are antihistamines, which dry the throat, thus compounding the problem.
- If you can identify the agent which sets off the allergic reaction, you may be able to avoid it. This is particularly the case with allergies to certain foodstuffs.

Asthma

The breathlessness caused by the constriction and inflammation of the bronchial tubes makes it very difficult to breathe, hence to speak.

Remedies:
- Again, seek medical help.
- Try to identify what sets off the attack – and avoid it.

Viral throat infections

Remedies:
- Seek medical advice.
- Rest your voice, using it as little as possible.
- Drink plenty of fluids (avoiding very hot or very cold drinks).
- Many people find the traditional treatment of warm water, honey and lemon juice helps to soothe the throat.
- In severe cases, it helps to make a steam inhalation (a bowl of boiling water which you inhale with a towel draped over your head). Some people put Vicks or some other mentholated product in the water. If you do this, you will need to drink a lot afterwards, as menthol is also a drying agent.

NB For all the above conditions it is well worth trying homeopathic medicine. You should only do this, however, after seeking the advice of a registered homeopathic practitioner. Homeopathic treatments have the advantage of cooperating with your body's natural processes; helping the body to help itself. They are also normally free of side-effects.

c) Throat clearing

The problem
- Feeling a need to clear the throat frequently, often as a result of throat infections. This is a sort of vicious circle – the more ticklish your throat, the more you want to clear it; the more you clear it, the more ticklish and sore it becomes.

Remedies:
- Avoid clearing your throat as far as possible.
- Keep a glass of water handy and sip it whenever you feel the urge to clear your throat.
- Try to swallow rather than clearing your throat.

d) Medicines

Many medicines are harmful to the voice. Cold remedies containing antihistamines, aspirin and caffeine tend to dry up the vocal tract, which exacerbates voice problems. Aspirin in particular should be avoided as it can cause haemorrhaging of the throat membranes, leading to soreness. Cough sweets and lozenges should likewise be avoided as far as possible. Fruit gums are better. Chewing gum is better still as it stimulates the production of saliva, which keeps the vocal tract well lubricated. If you do occasionally have to resort to patent medicines for immediate, short-term relief, make sure that you do not go on using them for too long. If your condition lasts for more than a week, however, you should seek medical advice anyway.

e) Hormonal changes

The problem
Apart from the normal changes in voice pitch and quality related to ageing, there may be some abnormal hormonal factors. Abnormally active or inactive adrenal, pituitary and thyroid glands can result in voices which sound excessively high or low pitched for the person producing them.

Remedies:
• Seek the advice of an endocrinologist.

f) Substance abuse

The three main substances with potential for causing voice problems are tobacco, alcohol and drugs. It is easy to sound sanctimonious when advising people to stay off these three substances, yet they are all primary enemies of the natural voice.

• Tobacco, apart from its proven carcinogenic properties, causes drying of the vocal tract. It may also bring about shortness of breath and chronic coughing, and heart disease.
• Alcohol dries the vocal tract, and it leads to loss of control over the voice muscles – the familiar slurred voice of the person who has had one too many.
• Long-term drug use has degenerative effects on the nervous system.
• Marihuana dries the throat.
• Cocaine causes chronic nose drip and deterioration of the mucous membranes.
• Drugs also lead to loss of muscular control, which affects the voice.

Remedies:
• If you don't smoke, drink, or take drugs, don't start.
• Stay away from smoky environments.
• If you are a habitual heavy smoker or drinker, try to cut down.
• If you are only a light or occasional social smoker or drinker, it shouldn't be too difficult to give it up entirely.

g) Dehydration

As we have already seen, any change in the moisture level in the air will have an effect on the voice. We need therefore to be careful to maintain our level of fluid intake, especially in hot or dry environments. The best indicator of whether your body is adequately hydrated is the colour of your urine! The paler it is, the better. In any case, make sure you drink plenty of water.

h) Tiredness

If we use our voices when we are tired, they will often be higher in pitch and lower in volume than usual. If we prolong use in these circumstances, the voice may develop more serious symptoms of strain. Teachers are peculiarly susceptible to tiring their voices because they are called upon to use them so much. What they can do is to avoid overusing their voices, and misusing them, for example by not shouting. (See *Self-induced problems* below.)

i) Fear, nerves, inhibitions

Many teachers, even after years of experience, still feel nervous when they have to confront a large group. If we are afraid or tense, we tend to raise our shoulders, which leads to constriction of the throat. We find it more difficult to breathe deeply, and our voices come out strained and high pitched.

3 Self-induced problems

'I know the enemy – and it is me.' (Gallwey 1997.) All too often, we behave in ways which are harmful to ourselves. Sometimes we do this through ignorance, because we don't know any better. However, there are times when we are at least half-aware that we are acting against our own best interests – yet we continue just the same! This section will draw attention to some of these problems. For many, the mention will be brief, since they have already been dealt with more fully elsewhere in this book.

a) Lifestyle

The axiom 'everything is connected' applies to the way we run our lives as well as to factors more obviously connected with the voice. An imbalance in diet or sleep patterns, for example, can have a knock-on effect on the voice (as well as on other aspects of our lives). Irregular and insufficient sleep will make your whole organism, including your voice, tired. If you are unfit, or seriously overweight, your breathing will be affected, and with it your voice. If your diet is wildly unbalanced (for instance by an over-reliance on junk and processed food, with no fresh fruit or vegetables), or if you eat at irregular intervals, especially late at night, you will almost certainly experience voice problems. 'Some vocal problems are related to indigestion.' (Rodenburg 1992.) If you wear tight clothing or footwear, this will have an effect on posture, as in the case of high-heeled shoes, or on breathing, as in the case of tightly-buttoned shirts and ties and tight belts. Noisy environments will cause you to raise your own volume to the detriment of your natural voice. And excessive levels of stress will cause muscular tension, especially in the jaw, tongue and shoulders/throat, all of which will have a negative effect on your voice.

b) Poor body use

Posture/alignment

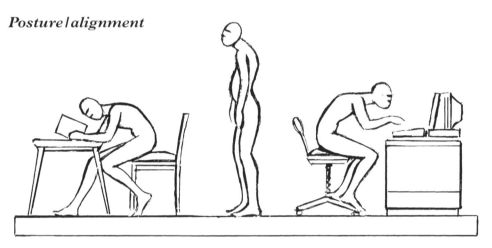

All the pioneers of body work, from Alexander onward, have assigned key importance to posture, where head, neck and spine are all in perfect alignment. If posture is maintained, everything else falls into place. And the reverse is also true, of course: if posture is off centre, things fall apart. If you habitually carry your head thrust forward, the neck muscles have to compensate, which leads to constriction in the throat. If you habitually pull back your head when speaking, the throat is again squeezed. If you develop a slouched posture, there will be problems with taking sufficient breath to support your voice.

Self-monitoring is your best protection. Check yourself from time to time each day both during and between lessons. If you find it helpful, learn and use the Alexander mental directions: 'Let my neck be free, to let my head go forward and up, to let my torso lengthen and widen, to let my legs release away from my torso, and let my shoulders widen.'

Muscular tension
This is most obvious and most harmful in the head, neck, shoulders and jaw. It may be the result of nervous tension or simply of having to maintain a constant body position over long periods. Whatever the cause, the effect is the same. If the shoulders are hunched and tense, the neck and chest are constricted, which impedes proper breathing. If the neck is held stiffly, muscular effort is being taken from where it is needed in order to compensate. If the jaw is tense, the mouth cavity cannot be used flexibly.

Again, your best approach is through regular self-monitoring, with simple remedial tactics. You can do shoulder-dropping movements for hunched shoulders, one or two head/neck rolls for neck tension, jaw massage and yawning for tension in the jaw and tongue.

Breathing

If breathing is too shallow, that is if the air is only drawn into the upper chest, there will be insufficient support for full and sustained voice use. Other breathing problems may come about if you allow emotional states, especially anger, to take over. Your breathing will then become uncontrolled and irregular, which will affect both the quantity and quality of your voice.

Regular monitoring to ensure that you are taking in a full measure of air can easily be done unobtrusively, even during class. Only you will notice it!

c) Overuse and misuse of the voice

Most teachers talk too much. Most teachers could talk a great deal less without it affecting the quality of their teaching. Silence and the use of conventionally agreed signals or gestures can replace a lot of the effort we customarily expend in words. If you teach for many hours in the day, you need to conserve your voice.

Using your voice in stressful environments is harmful. The most common stressful environment is a noisy classroom. Never try to talk over a noisy group: your voice will tire very quickly. Instead, find ways of reducing the noise level before you speak.

The most common forms of misuse include the following:

Talking too loudly or too softly

Both shouting and whispering are harmful to the voice. Both produce irritation and hoarseness if they are prolonged.

Hard glottal attack

This is particularly noticeable on words beginning with a vowel sound. Air pressure builds up behind the vocal cords just before the word is spoken. The air is then released with a pop and the sound explodes, projected forcibly out. The speaker comes across as someone over-emphasizing words.

> *The explosion of sound … is caused by the lack of synchronisation of the muscles of breathing and the muscles of speech, resulting in the vocal folds coming together with great force and this may, over a period of time, damage them.*
> Martin and Darnley

It is easily remedied. All you need to do is to get into the habit of exhaling on an 'h' before words beginning with a vowel: *h–apple*, *h–exercise*, etc. If you practise this for a bit (outside class!) you can soon simply 'think' the 'h' without actually sounding it.

'Pushing'

Rodenburg (1991) describes this:

> *The listener feels spoken 'at' not 'to'... The sound is typically nervous and overstressed. The tension suffered in the throat makes it impossible for the voice to achieve any range... At the crucial moment of vocalisation the breath and its support cannot get under the sound because it will not come. The speaker is left stranded with no reserve of power to draw on ... so he or she begins to push for power only from the throat and strains the vocal cords in the process. The energy needed to vocalise is 'head-butted' or kicked from the throat.*

She goes on to describe the 'pusher':

> *Habitual pushers will often go red in the face as they force sound out ... The head could jut forwards, veins will appear along the side of the neck as the pressure increases, the body will go off-centre and very little breath will be taken. These are the classic signs of the push.*

If you feel that you are pushing, the first thing to do is to relax shoulders, neck and jaw. Then establish a deep pattern of breathing. Then yawn and, as you complete the yawn, speak your words. All the time, relax and be aware of what you are saying. Tell yourself there is no need to push.

The 'pull back'

We sometimes describe it as 'swallowing our words' (Rodenburg 1991). Typically the sound gets into the mouth and then the speaker pulls it back into the throat. Sometimes this literally involves a pulling back of the head, thus trapping the sound in the throat. The best way to counter it is to practise getting the voice to the front of the mouth. Rodenburg also suggests visualizing the sound as coming out of the mouth in an arc, like water from a hose, travelling away from you towards an objective.

4   Some ideas for voice maintenance

Voice warm-ups

The purpose of these suggested workouts is to give you some very simple routines which can be done quickly, either just before you have to teach or lecture, or between classes to refresh you. They are not intended as full voice workouts, which are part of your ongoing voice maintenance.

Short version (5–10 minutes)

- Stand in the balanced position with your feet evenly spaced shoulder-width apart. Make sure your head is in alignment, with no neck or shoulder tension. Keep your knees slightly flexed, not locked.

- Raise your arms slowly from the sides to meet above the head on the in-breath, then lower them on the out-breath. Do this five times.

- Raise both arms above your head. Then drop forward from the waist till your head and arms are hanging loosely. Breathe as deeply as possible into your back. Feel the air stretching your back ribs. Take five long, slow breaths. Then come up slowly through the spine. Unroll your neck vertebrae last of all. Feel your head floating on the top of your spine.

- Raise both shoulders as high as you can, hold them for a moment, then let them drop back into place. Do this five times.

- Do a complete neck roll three times to the right and three times to the left. As you roll, hum a note. Stretch your tongue as far out of your mouth as you can. Then raise and lower the tip. Stretch your tongue like this five times.

- Keeping the tip of your tongue against your bottom teeth, make the sound *–eee*, tensing your tongue as much as you can. Then flatten your tongue on the floor of your mouth and make the sound *–ooo*.

- Make the sounds alternately for a few moments: *–eee –ooo –eee –ooo* …

- Keep your jaw relaxed and try not to move your lips, only your tongue. Push your lips out as far as they will go. Then stretch them as far as possible to the side. Do these movements alternately for a few moments.

- Do a big yawn three times to open up the back of your throat.

- Give your lips, tongue and soft palate some practice by rapidly speaking the sounds: *–ptk, –ptk* … *–bdg, –bdg* … *–ktp, –ktp* … *–gdb, –gdb* …

- Change the order of the sounds: *–tkp, –ktp*, etc.

- Gently massage your jaw joint, then massage gently downwards in a circular motion. Do this two or three times.

Longer version (approximately 15–20 minutes)

- Stand in the balanced position, as in the shorter version. Establish a regular deep breathing pattern. Put the backs of your hands on your bottom ribs at the back and feel them swing open as you breathe in. Bend your knees till you are in a half-sitting position.

- Check that your spine is erect and that head, neck and spine are in alignment. Put the back of your right hand on the palm of your left hand and hold them loosely in front of you at a point just below your navel. As you breathe in, raise your hands towards the front until they are above your head.

- At the same time, straighten your legs (but do not lock your knees). As your hands reach the point above your head, your legs should be straight, and your lungs should be full.

- Then separate your hands and sweep them down towards the sides on the out-breath, flexing your knees as you do so. Your lungs should be empty as you hit the bottom.

- Repeat this cycle eight times.

- Put your right hand under your left armpit and cross your left hand to grasp your right arm just below the shoulder. Hug yourself tightly as you breathe as low as possible into your back. Do this five times.

- Then drop forward from the waist, still hugging yourself, and take five deep breaths while you are down. Come up slowly on an in-breath. Then change arms: left hand under right armpit, etc, and repeat the cycle.

- Vacuum your lungs three times (see p 10).

- Do a sequence of three very deep sighs. Then six panting breaths. Then another three sighs. In each case, vocalize –*haa* for the sighs and –*huh* for the panting.

- Take a short rest, preferably lying in the semi-supine position (see p 2).

- Roll your right shoulder in a circle towards the front five times, then your left shoulder. Then roll each one five times towards the rear.

- Let your head fall back as far as it will comfortably go. Take a big breath and then exhale, making the sound –*haa* with your head still back.

- Use the whole of your breath before taking another. Do this three times.

- Then bring your head up so that you are looking directly ahead.

- Again, take a breath and make the sound –*ho*. When you need to, take a new breath. Do it three times.

- Let your head drop forward onto your chest, take a breath and make the sound –*hee*. Repeat this for three breaths as before.

- Do three headrolls to the right and three to the left on a hum, as in the short version.

- Do the tongue, lip and soft palate exercises as in the short version.

- Do three big yawns. Then yawn three times with your mouth closed.

- Smile three times with the back of your throat. Hold your lower jaw firmly with your hands. Then lift your upper jaw away from the lower jaw so that your lower jaw stays in the same place while your head moves back.

- Repeat this until your head is thrown way back. Then do it again.

- Massage your jaw as in the short version.

- Then make exaggerated chewing movements for a few moments. Add sound as you chew: *–aa, –ai, –au, –oo, –ee*. With your fingers, gently massage from the bridge of your nose diagonally across your cheeks on a hum. Do this five times.

- Do the pranayama breathing exercise (see p 54) in the ratio of six in to twelve out-breaths. Do eight complete cycles.

- Take a deep breath. Then make the sound *–aah*.

- Start as low in your range as you can and move up to the top of your range smoothly, without a pitch break. Then go down to the bottom again. Do this three times, taking breath as needed.

Take a short rest. You are now ready to start.

In this section, I have put forward suggestions for regular, short warm-ups. Do adapt them to your own preferences and circumstances. But also remember that there are key areas everyone needs to cover:

- overall posture and relaxation
- neck, head and shoulder tension
- opening up and controlling your breathing
- flexing your vocal organs – tongue, lips, jaw, soft palate
- bringing your voice up from deep inside you

Annotated bibliography

Books with a voice-training focus

Cicely Berry *The Actor and the Text*.
Virgin Books, London 1993
An inspirational and important book by the doyenne of British theatre voicework. See especially Chapters 1 and 2. Though this is written with actors in mind, in many cases simply replace 'actor' with 'teacher', and bingo! Chapters 11 and 12 have good practical exercises. Chapters 5 and 6 have exercises for Shakespearean texts but these can be adapted to any text. Excellent material on the exploration of words: their weight, texture, energy, and on rhythm and stress.

Oren L. Brown *Discover Your Voice: How to Develop Healthy Voice Habits*. Singular Publishing Group, San Diego, Calif. 1996
Very comprehensive treatment of all aspects of voice building. The exercises are clearly explained and useful. There is an accompanying audio CD.

Daniel R. Boone *Is Your Voice Telling on You?*
Singular Publishing Group, San Diego, Calif. 1991
A self-help book. The main focus is on trouble-shooting: what can go wrong and how to deal with it. Very practical and easy to read.

Stephen Chun Tao Cheng *The Tao of Voice*.
Destiny Books, Rochester, Vermont 1991
A very down-to-earth approach to the singing voice – but equally applicable to the speaking voice. There are some excellent and simple exercises, and recommendations for daily living. Highly recommended.

Kristin Linklater *Freeing the Natural Voice*.
Drama Book Publishers, New York 1976
One of the standard texts used on voice-training courses. A very thorough introduction to all aspects of voicework; contains detailed descriptions of a whole programme of exercises.

Kristin Linklater *Freeing Shakespeare's Voice*.
Theatre Communications Group, New York 1992
An approach to the performance of Shakespeare's texts, with emphasis on restoring the physicality of Shakespeare's language. The many useful exercises can be adapted by language teachers for work on other texts. See especially Chapters 3 and 4.

Michael McCallion *The Voice Book*.
Faber and Faber, London 1988
An excellent, comprehensive introduction to voicework. Though this was written primarily for actors, it can be used by anyone. Good practical exercises. Highly recommended.

Stephanie Martin and Lyn Darnley *The Voice Sourcebook*. Winslow Press, Bicester, Oxon 1992
A large format book with very useful photocopiable exercises on all aspects of voicework. Very practical and untechnical. Highly recommended.

Stephanie Martin and Lyn Darnley *The Teaching Voice*. Whurr Publishers, London 1996
This book is mainly concerned with the harm done to teachers' voices (in the UK) by sustained misuse. Though it is very UK-centric (and L1 centred), there are useful exercises in Chapters 10 and 11.

Malcolm Morrison *Clear Speech*.
A & C Black, London 1989
A very compact self-help manual. It focuses exclusively on 'faults' and exercises to remedy them. Useful and accessible.

Patsy Rodenburg *The Right to Speak*.
Methuen, London 1991
An outspoken, polemical, passionate book in defence of everyone's right to a voice by the Head of Voice at the Royal National Theatre and the Guildhall School of Speech and Drama in London. Part 1 is especially interesting for its critique of habitual behaviours, both physical and mental. In Part 2 there are excellent practical exercises on relaxation, breathwork and placing the voice.

Patsy Rodenburg *The Need for Words*.
Methuen, London 1993
In Part 1 there is a characteristically vigorous and punchy plea for the restitution of oracy. In Part 2, Chapter 4 gives an effective set of exercises for relaxation, breathing and voicing. Chapter 5 contains useful ideas for working with texts.

Patsy Rodenburg *The Actor Speaks*. Methuen, London 1998

> The distillation of her long experience in training and coaching actors. She offers a seven-stage programme. Stages 1 (*Basics of voicework*), 2 (*Resonance, range and speech*) and 3 (*Opening up texts*) are the most useful for language teachers, who will find many ideas to exploit.

Books with a focus on physical well-being

There are many books describing the Alexander Technique. This is a small selection. Remember, however, that the Alexander Technique is not a set of physical exercises, and for real benefits you need to take lessons with an accredited Alexander Technique teacher. (See useful addresses.)

Sarah Barker *The Alexander Technique*. Bantam Books, Toronto and New York 1978

> A brief and clear manual.

Michael Gelb *Body Learning: An Introduction to the Alexander Technique*. Aurum Press, London 1994

> This is one of the clearest accounts of the Alexander Technique and its principles. Highly recommended.

Judith Leibowitz and Bill Connington *The Alexander Technique*. Mandarin Paperbacks, London 1991

> In Part 1 the Alexander Technique is clearly described. In Part 2 the Leibowitz procedures, a set of simple movements based on the Alexander Technique, are set out, then applied to daily activities and to sports.

Glen Park *The Art of Changing: A New Approach to the Alexander Technique*. Ashgrove Press, Bath 1989

> In Part 1 the Alexander Technique is thoroughly described. In Part 2 there is an attempt to relate the approach to energy flows, the chakras and other esoteric systems, thus integrating the Alexander Technique with the 'whole person'. There is an accompanying audio cassette.

Chris Stevens *The Alexander Technique*. Macdonald Optima, London 1987

> A very straightforward description of the technique: what it is, why we need it, how it works. There are suggestions for self-help.

Books on systems similar to the Alexander Technique but with distinct features of their own:

Mary Bond *Rolfing Movement Integration: A Self-help Approach to Balancing the Body*. Healing Arts Press, Rochester, Vermont 1993

> A description of the system developed by Dr Ida Rolf. It focuses on the effects of habit on posture; gravity and the body; breathing and visualization, working on small parts of the body systematically, one at a time. There are detailed exercises. Contains many useful addresses for those wishing to follow it up.

Y. P. Dong *Still as a Mountain, Powerful as Thunder: Simple Taoist Exercises for Healing, Vitality and Peace of Mind*. Shambhala Publications, Boston, Mass. 1993

> Very simple to do exercises with clear instructions and photographic illustrations. The exercises are for general well-being as well as for specific ailments. A no-nonsense approach.

Moshe Feldenkrais *Awareness Through Movement: Health Exercises for Personal Growth*. Penguin, London 1980

> The principles and rationale for the Feldenkrais method are clearly explained in the first part of the book. There are then twelve illustrated lessons, each focusing on different areas of the body. The method explores the body–mind connection in detail. The exercises result in heightened body/self awareness and increased vitality. Highly recommended.

Books with a focus on therapeutic/spiritual dimensions

Not everyone will find themselves in sympathy with many of the approaches dealt with by books in this section. They may seem too mystical or even plain daft. However, there is a growing body of evidence to show that such approaches do have positive effects. They cannot simply be written off as part of the lunatic fringe.

Chris B. Brewer and Don G. Campbell *Rhythms of Learning*. Zephyr Press, Arizona 1991

Don G. Campbell *The Roar of Silence: Healing Powers of Breath, Tone and Music*. The Theosophical Publishing House, Wheaton, Illinois 1989
> An introduction to toning. Highly recommended.

Olivea Dewhurst-Maddock *Healing with Sound: Self-help Techniques Using Music and Your Voice*. Gaia Books, London 1997
> A very sensible and informative treatment of the nature of sound, hearing and the voice with practical exercises and illustrations. Highly recommended.

W. Timothy Gallwey *The Inner Game of Tennis*. Pan, London 1997
> This is not just about tennis! It is essentially about learning to let go, to achieve 'effortless effort' by purging ourselves of the relentless urge to cripple ourselves with self-criticism.

Kay Gardner *Sounding the Inner Landscape: Music as Medicine*. Element Books, Shaftesbury, Dorset 1997

Laeh M. Garfield *Sound Medicine: Healing with Music, Voice and Song*. Celestial Arts Publishing Berkeley, Calif. 1987

Jonathan Goldman *Healing Sounds: the Power of Harmonics*. Element Books, Shaftesbury, Dorset 1992

Benjamin Hoff *The Tao of Pooh*. Penguin, London 1982
> Like the Gallwey book, it has no explicit connection with voicework – but can be powerfully applied to it.

Will Johnson *The Posture of Meditation*. Shambhala Publications, Boston, Mass. 1996
> The simplest, clearest and briefest account I have found of sitting meditation. Highly recommended.

W.A. Mathieu *The Listening Book*. Shambhala Publications, Boston, Mass. 1991
> This is about developing sensitivity to the world of sound outside (and inside) ourselves, and learning how to enter into it.

Paul Newham *The Singing Cure: an Introduction to Voice Movement Therapy*. Shambhala Publications, Boston, Mass. 1994

Paul Newham *Therapeutic Voicework*. Jessica Kingsley Publishers, London 1998
> Chapters 7, *The Healing Voice*, 9, *The Dramatic Voice* and 11, *Voice, Breath and Body* are the most relevant.

Pauline Taylor and Katie Head *Readings in Teacher Development*. Heinemann, Oxford 1997
> See especially Chapter 6, *Supporting yourself*.

Paul Wilson *Instant Calm*. Penguin, London 1995
> One hundred practical techniques for inducing calm and well-being. Highly recommended.

Other useful books

Related to EFL pronunciation teaching

Val Black, Maggie McNorton, Angie Malderez and Sue Parker *Speaking: Advanced*. Oxford University Press, Oxford 1992

Barbara Bradford *Intonation in Context*. Cambridge University Press, Cambridge 1988
Many of the activities can double as voicework.

A. Brown (ed) *Teaching English Pronunciation: a book of readings*. Routledge, London 1991

A. Brown (ed) *Approaches to Pronunciation Teaching*. Macmillan/MEP in association with the British Council, London 1992

Christine Dalton and Barbara Seidlhofer *Pronunciation*. Oxford University Press, Oxford 1994

J. B. Gilbert *Clear Speech: Pronunciation and Listening Comprehension in American English*. Cambridge University Press, Cambridge 1993

Clement Laroy *Pronunciation*. Oxford University Press, Oxford 1995

Rob Nolasco and Lois Arthur *Conversation*. Oxford University Press, Oxford 1987

Adrian Underhill *Sound Foundations*. Macmillan Heinemann ELT, Oxford 1994

Michael Vaughan-Rees *Rhymes and Rhythm*. Macmillan, Basingstoke, Hants 1994

Related to theatre work

Clive Barker *Theatre Games*. Methuen, London 1977
Chapters 13 and 14 are especially relevant to voicework.

Anthony Frost and Ralph Yarrow *Improvisation in Drama*. Macmillan, Basingstoke, Hants 1990

Keith Johnstone *Impro: Improvisation and the Theatre*. Methuen, London 1989

Alan Maley and Alan Duff *Drama Techniques in Language Learning*. Cambridge University Press, Cambridge 1982

Charlyn Wessels *Drama*. Oxford University Press, Oxford 1987
Many useful activities, especially in Chapters 4 and 5.

Related to poetry and storytelling

Christabel Burniston and Jocelyn Bell *Into the Life of Things: an exploration of language through verbal dynamics*. The English Speaking Board, Southport, Lancs 1972

Philip Davies Roberts *How Poetry Works*. Penguin, London 1986

Bernard Dufeu *Teaching Myself*. Oxford University Press, Oxford 1994

Rex Gibson *Teaching Shakespeare*. Cambridge University Press, Cambridge 1998
See especially Chapter 9, *Active Methods*.

Carolyn Graham *Jazz Chants*. Oxford University Press, New York 1978

Carolyn Graham *Jazz Chants for Children*. Oxford University Press, New York 1979

Mike Hayhoe and Stephen Parker *Words Large as Apples: Teaching Poetry 11–18*. Cambridge University Press, Cambridge 1988

Betty Rosen *And None of It Was Nonsense: The Power of Storytelling in School*. Mary Glasgow Publishers, London 1988

Betty Rosen *Shapers and Polishers: Teachers as Storytellers*. Collins Educational, London 1993

Andrew Wright *Storytelling With Children*. Oxford University Press, Oxford 1996

Andrew Wright *Creating Stories with Children*. Oxford University Press, Oxford 1997

Useful addresses

Professional associations/centres

British Voice Association
35/43 Lincoln's Inn Fields
London WC2A 3PN UK

Voice Care Network UK
29 Southbank Road
Kenilworth
Warwicks CV8 1LA UK

Society of Teachers of Speech
and Drama
73 Berry Hill Road
Mansfield
Notts NG18 4RU UK

Royal College of Speech and
Language Therapists
7 Bath Place
Rivington Street
London EC2A 3DR UK

British Performing Arts Medicine Trust
18 Ogle Street
London W1P 7LG UK

British Society for Music Therapy
25 Rosslyn Avenue
East Barnet
Herts EN4 8DH UK

Tomatis Centre UK Ltd
3 Wallands Crescent
Lewes
E. Sussex BN7 2QT UK

Voice Movement Therapy
International Head Office
PO Box 4218
London SE22 0JE UK

National Center for Voice and Speech
Wendell Johnson Speech and Hearing
Center
The University of Iowa
Iowa City
IA 52242 USA

Globe Theatre
New Globe Walk
Bankside
London SE1 9DT UK

Centres with an educational focus

Education Department
The Royal National Theatre
Upper ground
South Bank
London SE1 9PX UK

Royal Shakespeare Company
Education Department
Waterside
Stratford-upon-Avon
Warwicks CV36 6BB UK

IATEFL Pronunciation SIG
3 Kingsdown Chambers
Kingsdown Park
Whitstable
Kent CT5 2FL UK

SEAL (Society for Effective and
Affective Learning)
PO Box 2246
Bath BA1 2YR UK

Centres promoting special methods

Society of Teachers of the Alexander
Technique
20 London House
266 Fulham Road
London SW10 9EL UK

North American Society of Teachers of
the Alexander Technique
PO Box 3992
Champaign
IL 61826–3992 USA

North American Society of Teachers
of the Alexander Technique
PO Box 806
Ansonia Station
New York
NY 10023–9998 USA

Australian Society of Teachers of the
Alexander Technique
PO Box 529
Milson's Point
NSW 2061 Australia

Feldenkrais Guild
524 Ellsworth Street
PO Box 489
Albany
OR 97321–0143 USA

Feldenkrais International Training
Centre
PO Box 1207
Hove
E. Sussex BN3 2GG UK

New Age centres

School for Body–Mind Centering
189 Pondview Drive
Amherst
MA 01002 USA

Rolf Institute
302 Pearl Street
PO Box 1868
Boulder
CO 80306–1868 USA

Tao of Voice Center
395 Riverside Drive
Box 7A
New York
NY 10025 USA

Sound Healers Association
PO Box 2240
Boulder
CO 80306 USA

Olivea Dewhurst-Maddock
Healing with Sound Workshop
47 Kentsford Road
Kents Bank
Cumbria LA11 7BB UK

Publishers and record companies

Element Books Ltd
Longmead
Shaftesbury
Dorset UK

Shambhala Publications Inc
Horticultural Hall
300 Massachusetts Avenue
Boston
MA 02115–4544 USA

The Theosophical Publishing House
PO Box 270
Wheaton
IL 60189–0270 USA

The Librarian
Institute for Music, Health and Education
PO Box 1244
Boulder
CO 80306 USA

Ladyslipper Records Inc
PO Box 3124
Durham
NC 27715 USA

Cold Mountain Music
PO Box 912
Sebastopol
CA 95473 USA

New Age Classics
18 Hopefield Avenue
London NW6 6LH UK

Index

Index of quoted authors